11/03/45
22.45

GLOBAL RESOURCES

Opposing Viewpoints®

Helen Cothran, *Book Editor*

Daniel Leone, *President*
Bonnie Szumski, *Publisher*
Scott Barbour, *Managing Editor*

OPPOSING
VIEWPOINTS®
SERIES

GREENHAVEN
PRESS®

THOMSON
—————✦—————™
GALE

San Diego • Detroit • New York • San Francisco • Cleveland
New Haven, Conn. • Waterville, Maine • London • Munich

THOMSON
GALE

LIBRARY OF CONGRESS   ON DATA
Global resources / Helen Cothran, book editor.
    p. cm. — (Opposing viewpoints series)
Includes bibliographical references and index.
ISBN 0-7377-1682-7 (pbk. : alk. paper) — ISBN 0-7377-1681-9 (lib. : alk. paper)
    1. Economic development—Environmental aspects. 2. Natural
resources—Management. 3. Conservation of natural resources. I. Cothran,
Helen. II. Opposing viewpoints series (Unnumbered)
HD75.6G555 2003
333.7—dc21   2002041629

Printed in the United States of America

"Congress shall make
no law. . . abridging the
freedom of speech, or of
the press."

First Amendment to the U.S. Constitution

The basic foundation of our democracy is the First
Amendment guarantee of freedom of expression.
The Opposing Viewpoints Series is dedicated to the
concept of this basic freedom and the idea that it is
more important to practice it than to enshrine it.

Contents

Why Consider Opposing Viewpoints?

"The only way in which a human being can make some approach to knowing the whole of a subject is by hearing what can be said about it by persons of every variety of opinion and studying all modes in which it can be looked at by every character of mind. No wise man ever acquired his wisdom in any mode but this."

John Stuart Mill

In our media-intensive culture it is not difficult to find differing opinions. Thousands of newspapers and magazines and dozens of radio and television talk shows resound with differing points of view. The difficulty lies in deciding which opinion to agree with and which "experts" seem the most credible. The more inundated we become with differing opinions and claims, the more essential it is to hone critical reading and thinking skills to evaluate these ideas. Opposing Viewpoints books address this problem directly by presenting stimulating debates that can be used to enhance and teach these skills. The varied opinions contained in each book examine many different aspects of a single issue. While examining these conveniently edited opposing views, readers can develop critical thinking skills such as the ability to compare and contrast authors' credibility, facts, argumentation styles, use of persuasive techniques, and other stylistic tools. In short, the Opposing Viewpoints Series is an ideal way to attain the higher-level thinking and reading skills so essential in a culture of diverse and contradictory opinions.

In addition to providing a tool for critical thinking, Opposing Viewpoints books challenge readers to question their own strongly held opinions and assumptions. Most people form their opinions on the basis of upbringing, peer pressure, and personal, cultural, or professional bias. By reading carefully balanced opposing views, readers must directly confront new ideas as well as the opinions of those with whom they disagree. This is not to simplistically argue that everyone who reads opposing views will—or should—change his or her opinion. Instead, the series enhances readers' understanding of their own views by encouraging confrontation with opposing ideas. Careful examination of others' views can lead to the readers' understanding of the logical inconsistencies in their own opinions, perspective on why they hold an opinion, and the consideration of the possibility that their opinion requires further evaluation.

Evaluating Other Opinions

To ensure that this type of examination occurs, Opposing Viewpoints books present all types of opinions. Prominent spokespeople on different sides of each issue as well as well-known professionals from many disciplines challenge the reader. An additional goal of the series is to provide a forum for other, less known, or even unpopular viewpoints. The opinion of an ordinary person who has had to make the decision to cut off life support from a terminally ill relative, for example, may be just as valuable and provide just as much insight as a medical ethicist's professional opinion. The editors have two additional purposes in including these less known views. One, the editors encourage readers to respect others' opinions—even when not enhanced by professional credibility. It is only by reading or listening to and objectively evaluating others' ideas that one can determine whether they are worthy of consideration. Two, the inclusion of such viewpoints encourages the important critical thinking skill of objectively evaluating an author's credentials and bias. This evaluation will illuminate an author's reasons for taking a particular stance on an issue and will aid in readers' evaluation of the author's ideas.

It is our hope that these books will give readers a deeper understanding of the issues debated and an appreciation of the complexity of even seemingly simple issues when good and honest people disagree. This awareness is particularly important in a democratic society such as ours in which people enter into public debate to determine the common good. Those with whom one disagrees should not be regarded as enemies but rather as people whose views deserve careful examination and may shed light on one's own.

Thomas Jefferson once said that "difference of opinion leads to inquiry, and inquiry to truth." Jefferson, a broadly educated man, argued that "if a nation expects to be ignorant and free . . . it expects what never was and never will be." As individuals and as a nation, it is imperative that we consider the opinions of others and examine them with skill and discernment. The Opposing Viewpoints Series is intended to help readers achieve this goal.

David L. Bender and Bruno Leone,
Founders

Greenhaven Press anthologies primarily consist of previously published material taken from a variety of sources, including periodicals, books, scholarly journals, newspapers, government documents, and position papers from private and public organizations. These original sources are often edited for length and to ensure their accessibility for a young adult audience. The anthology editors also change the original titles of these works in order to clearly present the main thesis of each viewpoint and to explicitly indicate the opinion presented in the viewpoint. These alterations are made in consideration of both the reading and comprehension levels of a young adult audience. Every effort is made to ensure that Greenhaven Press accurately reflects the original intent of the authors included in this anthology.

Introduction

"Among the environmental specters confronting humanity in the 21st century . . . a shortage of fresh water is at the top of the list."

—Fen Montaigne, National Geographic

American writer and humorist Mark Twain once quipped, "whiskey's for drinking, water's for fighting about." He had in mind the battles being waged in the American Southwest in the late 1800s over scarce water supplies, wars that continue to this day. California, for example, continues to take a disproportionate share of water from the Colorado River, on which many western states depend for their freshwater needs. Needless to say, the Golden State's thirst has not made it popular among its neighbors.

The fight for water is not confined to the southwestern United States, nor is it the only resource battled over. Indeed, water scarcity, along with the depletion of other resources such as petroleum reserves and grazing lands, will inevitably increase friction not only within nations but between nations as well. The issues surrounding water scarcity can serve as an illustration of why global resources in general are becoming an ever-growing concern.

Ismail Serageldin, vice president of the World Bank, predicted in 1995, "Many of the wars of [the twentieth] century were about oil—but the wars of the next century will be about water." Many experts contend that most of those wars will likely occur in the Middle East. The region's growing population will continue to drain underground aquifers, a serious concern in a predominantly arid land. In the disputed area of the West Bank, for example, Jewish and Palestinian settlers—notorious combatants—share a reliance on the Yargon-Tanninim aquifer, a situation ripe for conflict. Battles over shrinking water supplies are rooted in unassailable scientific facts and human population dynamics.

Although the "Blue Planet" has plenty of water, most of it is located in the world's oceans. Of the earth's total water supply, 97.5 percent is salt water, which is essentially unusable for drinking and irrigation. Only 2.5 percent of Earth's water is fresh. Of that amount, 68.7 percent is frozen in glaciers and permafrost, and another 30.1 percent is located in the ground, most deep within the earth's crust. That leaves only 0.4 percent as surface water, such as rivers and lakes, and atmospheric water, such as clouds.

The limited amount of freshwater available to the world's people is becoming a serious concern as the human population grows. Experts predict that the world's population will grow from 6 billion in 2002 to 9 billion in 2050, exacerbating existing water problems. Today, an estimated 1.2 billion people drink unclean water, and about 2.5 billion lack proper toilets or sewage systems. These facts have fatal consequences. *National Geographic* reports that every twenty minutes, "eighty children around the world will die because they didn't have enough clean water or sanitation facilities. In one day, 9,300 people will have perished from diarrhea, cholera, . . . and other diseases spread by contaminated water or the lack of water for adequate hygiene."

As the human population grows, so too must agricultural production to feed the world's people, but many experts claim that diminishing water supplies will make that increasingly difficult. Sixty-nine percent of all freshwater is used to irrigate crops. As nations have stepped up crop production to feed their increasing populations, water supplies have been drastically reduced. Governments have compounded the problem by subsidizing irrigation water to encourage farmers to grow more food, but the practice hastens water depletion. As advances in agricultural practices have increased the world's production of grain, farmers have begun relying more heavily on underground aquifers for irrigation water. Unfortunately, in many regions of the world, people are extracting more from the water table than can be replenished via rainfall. Moreover, many underground water sources are "fossil aquifers," which are remnants of ancient climates that were far wetter than current conditions. Pumping from fossil aquifers eventually exhausts them.

Many regions around the world are experiencing serious problems as a result of diminishing water supplies. Northern China is running a chronic water deficit. Like India, China's overuse of its freshwater supply has boosted food production, but the gains are proving short-lived. Eventually, worsening groundwater deficits may require Chinese farmers to stop irrigating some of their lands. In the 1970s, the government of Saudi Arabia subsidized large-scale wheat production in the desert. Unfortunately, Saudi irrigation consumed far more water than was naturally replenished, and many experts predict that the region's groundwater reserves will run out by 2040, if not sooner. The United States, too, faces serious water problems. By far the most worrisome is occurring in America's "bread basket," the food-producing states of the Great Plains. Irrigation for crops draws from the region's huge Ogallala aquifer, which gets very little replenishment from rainfall. The aquifer is currently being depleted at the rate of 12 billion cubic meters per year, or a total depletion volume equal to the annual flow of eighteen Colorado Rivers.

Many solutions, both technical and political, are being proposed to address growing water scarcity. Farmers in the High Plains area of the United States have begun using "surge systems," which deliver irrigation water to crops in a series of pulses rather than in a continuous stream. Less water runs off unused with this irrigation method, improving irrigation efficiency by 20 percent. Even more efficient are drip irrigation systems, which deliver water right to the roots of plants. Drip irrigation has a typical efficiency rate of 95 percent. These new irrigation methods are often used in tandem with sophisticated computerized probes that test soil moisture on a regular basis and then transmit the data to the farm's computers. Many solutions offered to solve water problems must be implemented by governments. For example, many environmentalists are urging governments to stop subsidizing inefficient irrigation practices and tax them instead.

Mark Twain, in commenting on the American Southwest, was more prophetic than he probably imagined. Battles fought over water resources—indeed, over most global resources—have only intensified since his time. The authors in *Global Resources: Opposing Viewpoints* discuss many of the resources that have given nations cause for concern in the following chapters: Are Global Resources Being Depleted?

What Agricultural Policies Should Be Pursued? What Energy Sources Should Be Pursued? How Can Global Resources Be Protected? In the debate about global resources, one fact remains incontrovertible: The "Blue Planet" contains a finite number of resources needed by growing numbers of people.

CHAPTER 1

Are Global Resources Being Depleted?

Chapter Preface

Scientist and writer Arthur C. Clarke once said that it was "inappropriate to call this planet Earth, when clearly it is ocean." Indeed, the ocean covers more than 70 percent of the earth's surface and contains more than 90 percent of the planet's habitats. The ocean also supplies people with nearly 100 million tons of fish annually. As writer Mary Anna Grove puts it, "The ocean is the lifeblood of our planet." Unfortunately, according to many scientists, the ocean is in trouble.

The National Oceanic and Atmospheric Administration claims that up to 75 percent of global fish stocks are overfished. Many environmentalists believe that overfishing is the greatest threat to the health of the oceans, and assert that as much as a third of the world's known fish species are threatened with extinction. The Ocean Conservancy issued a report in July 2002 stating that "overfishing not only threatens the world's food supply but can also bring about irreversible changes in marine biodiversity." University of British Columbia scientists contend that the global fish catch has declined by as much as 660,000 tons annually since 1988.

Overfishing is not the only factor threatening the earth's oceans, however. Development and pollution also play a role in decimating fish stocks. As coastlines are developed, more than twenty thousand acres of marine habitat are paved over each year. In addition, more than half the world's coral reefs are threatened by pollution. Another kind of pollution, the release of non-native species into the seas by cargo ships emptying ballast water, also leads to a rapid decline in marine life as foreign species take over. Another pollution-related problem is that open water, top-of-the-food-chain species such as tuna have become increasingly contaminated by mercury. In fact, a Food and Drug Administration (FDA) advisory committee has recommended that the FDA advise pregnant women not to eat tuna due to the danger mercury poses to fetuses.

Despite the many threats to the world's seas, attempts to protect marine life have been successful. The United Nations has adopted several resolutions against overfishing, such as its 1993 ban on drift-net fishing, a practice that indiscriminately kills any fish or mammal entrapped in the huge nets. In 1996, the U.S. Congress passed the Sustainable Fisheries Act, which reduced by half the number of permitted fishing days at sea, closed more than five thousand square miles of U.S. fishing grounds, and required the use of wider-mesh nets to allow young fish to escape. The United States has also expanded marine protection areas, or MPAs, which are closed to certain types of commercial fishing or prohibit fishing altogether. Another approach to declining fisheries is aquaculture, the cultivation of aquatic plants and animals. While aquaculture can help restock and protect sea animals, many critics claim that the practice also harms the environment by polluting nearby waterways with bacteria and other contaminants.

Some conservationists argue that the best way to protect the oceans is to stop eating fish altogether. Sylvia Earle, former chief scientist of the National Oceanic and Atmospheric Administration, contends, "Fish are not just lumps of meat waiting to be turned into steaks with a wedge of butter. What we're doing to them is unforgivable." It is unlikely that people will stop looking to the ocean for food, but as the world's human population grows, the need to use ocean food resources wisely has become increasingly important. The authors in the following chapter discuss other resources that are being depleted, such as rain forests and oil fields.

"The world's production of crude oil will fall, never to rise again."

Global Oil Reserves Are Being Exhausted

Kenneth S. Deffeyes

Kenneth S. Deffeyes contends in the following viewpoint that the world is facing a serious oil crisis. Using the same analytical methods that M. King Hubbert used in 1956 to determine that U.S. oil production would peak in the 1970s—referred to as Hubbert's Peak—Deffeyes calculates that global oil production will peak sometime between 2004 and 2008 and will then fall. According to Deffeyes, despite the fact that declining oil production threatens economies worldwide, the petroleum industry and U.S. politicians refuse to acknowledge the impending crisis. He recommends developing alternative energy sources before disaster strikes. Kenneth S. Deffeyes is professor emeritus at Princeton University.

As you read, consider the following questions:

1. In Deffeyes's opinion, what are two of the reasons that critics reject Hubbert's oil prediction?
2. Why does Deffeyes think that new technology will not avert the oil crisis?
3. According to the author, why is drilling in the South China Sea problematic?

Global oil production will probably reach a peak sometime during this decade. After the peak, the world's production of crude oil will fall, never to rise again. The world will not run out of energy, but developing alternative energy sources on a large scale will take at least 10 years. The slowdown in oil production may already be beginning; price fluctuations for crude oil and natural gas may be the preamble to a major crisis.

The Hubbert Prediction

In 1956, the geologist M. King Hubbert predicted that U.S. oil production would peak in the early 1970s. Almost everyone, inside and outside the oil industry, rejected Hubbert's analysis. The controversy raged until 1970, when the U.S. production of crude oil started to fall. Hubbert was right.

Around 1995, several analysts began applying Hubbert's method to world oil production, and most of them estimate that the peak year for world oil will be between 2004 and 2008. These analyses were reported in some of the most widely circulated sources: *Nature*, *Science*, and *Scientific American*. None of our political leaders seem to be paying attention. If the predictions are correct, there will be enormous effects on the world economy. Even the poorest nations need fuel to run irrigation pumps. The industrialized nations will be bidding against one another for the dwindling oil supply. The good news is that we will put less carbon dioxide into the atmosphere. The bad news is that my pickup truck has a 25-gallon tank.

The experts are making their 2004–8 predictions by building on Hubbert's pioneering work. Hubbert made his 1956 prediction at a meeting of the American Petroleum Institute in San Antonio, where he predicted that U.S. oil production would peak in the early 1970s. He said later that the Shell Oil head office was on the phone right down to the last five minutes before the talk, asking Hubbert to withdraw his prediction. Hubbert had an exceedingly combative personality, and he went through with his announcement.

I went to work in 1958 at the Shell research lab in Houston, where Hubbert was the star of the show. He had extensive scientific accomplishments in addition to his oil prediction. His belligerence during technical arguments gave rise to a saying around the lab, "That Hubbert is a bastard, but at least he's *our* bastard." Luckily, I got off to a good start with Hubbert; he remained a good friend for the rest of his life.

The Critics

Critics had many different reasons for rejecting Hubbert's oil prediction. Some were simply emotional; the oil business was highly profitable, and many people did not want to hear that the party would soon be over. A deeper reason was that many false prophets had appeared before. From 1900 onward, several of these people had divided the then known U.S. oil reserves by the annual rate of production. (Barrels of reserves divided by barrels per year gives an answer in years.) The typical answer was 10 years. Each of these forecasters started screaming that the U.S. petroleum industry would die in 10 years. They cried "wolf." During each ensuing 10 years, more oil reserves were added, and the industry actually grew instead of drying up. In 1956, many critics thought that Hubbert was yet another false prophet. Up through 1970, those who were following the story divided into pro-Hubbert and anti-Hubbert factions. One pro-Hubbert publication had the wonderful title "This Time the Wolf Really *Is* at the Door."

Hubbert's 1956 analysis tried out two different educated guesses for the amount of U.S. oil that would eventually be discovered and produced by conventional means: 150 billion and 200 billion barrels. He then made plausible estimates of future oil production rates for each of the two guesses. Even the more optimistic estimate, 200 billion barrels, led to a predicted peak of U.S. oil production in the early 1970s. The actual peak year turned out to be 1970.

Today, we can do something similar for world oil production. One educated guess of ultimate world recovery, 1.8 trillion barrels, comes from a 1997 country-by-country evaluation by Colin J. Campbell, an independent oil-industry consultant. In 1982, Hubbert's last published paper contained a world estimate of 2.1 trillion barrels. Hubbert's 1956 method leads to a peak year of 2001 for the 1.8-trillion-barrel estimate and a peak year of 2003 or 2004 for 2.1 trillion barrels. The prediction based on 1.8 trillion barrels makes a better match to the most recent 10 years of world production. . . .

Crisis? What Crisis?

A permanent and irreversible decline in world oil production would have both economic and psychological effects. So who is paying attention? The news media tell us that increases in energy prices are caused by an assortment of regulations, taxes, and distribution problems. During the election campaign of 2000, none of the presidential candidates told us that the sky was about to fall. The public attention to the predicted oil shortfall is essentially zero.

In private, the Organization of Petroleum Exporting Countries (OPEC) oil ministers probably know about the articles in *Science, Nature,* and *Scientific American.* Detailed articles, with contrasting opinions, have been published frequently in the *Oil and Gas Journal.* Crude oil prices have doubled in 2000. I suspect that OPEC knows that a global oil shortage may be only a few years away. The OPEC countries can trickle out just enough oil to keep the world economies functioning until that glorious day when they can market their remaining oil at mind-boggling prices.

"Hubbert's Peak"

The 100-year period when most of the world's oil will be produced is known as "Hubbert's peak." On this scale, the geologic time needed to form the oil resources can be visualized by extending the line five miles to the left.

It is not clear whether the major oil companies are facing up to the problem. Most of them display a business-as-usual facade. My limited attempts at spying turned up nothing useful. A company taking the 2004–8 hypothesis seriously would be willing to pay top dollar for existing oil fields. There does not seem to be an orgy of reserve acquisitions in progress.

Internally, the oil industry has an unusual psychology. Exploring for oil is an inherently discouraging activity. Nine out of 10 exploration wells are dry holes. Only one in a hundred exploration wells discovers an important oil field. Darwinian selection is involved: only the incurable optimists stay. They tell each other stories about a Texas county that started with 30 dry holes yet the next well was a major discovery. "Never is heard a discouraging word." A permanent drop in world oil production beginning in this decade is definitely a discouraging word.

No Way Out

Is there any way out? Is there some way the crisis could be averted?

New Technology. One of the responses in the 1980s was to ask for a double helping of new technology. Here is the problem: before 1995 (when the dot.com era began), the oil industry earned a higher rate of return on invested capital than any other industry. When oil companies tried to use some of their earnings to diversify, they discovered that everything else was less profitable than oil. Their only investment option was doing research to make their own exploration and production operations even more profitable. Billions of dollars went into petroleum technology development, and much of the work was successful. That makes it difficult to ask today for new technology. Most of those wheels have already been invented.

Drill Deeper. There is an "oil window" that depends on subsurface temperatures. The rule of thumb says that temperatures 7,500 feet down are hot enough to "crack" organic-rich sediments into oil molecules. However, beyond 15,000 feet the rocks are so hot that the oil molecules are further cracked into natural gas. The range from 7,000 to 15,000 feet is called the "oil window." If you drill deeper than 15,000 feet, you can find natural gas but little oil. Drilling rigs capable of penetrating to 15,000 feet became available in 1938.

Drill Someplace New. Geologists have gone to the ends of the Earth in their search for oil. The only rock outcrops in the jungle are in the banks of rivers and streams; geologists waded up the streams picking leeches off their legs. A typical field geologist's comment about jungle, desert, or tundra was: "She's medium-tough country." As an example, at the very northernmost tip of Alaska, at Point Barrow, the United States set up Naval Petroleum Reserve #4 in 1923. As early as 1923, somebody knew that the Arctic Slope of Alaska would be a major oil producer.

Today, about the only promising petroleum province that remains unexplored is part of the South China Sea, where exploration has been delayed by a political problem. International law divides oil ownership at sea along lines halfway between the adjacent coastlines. A valid claim to an island in the ocean pushes the boundary out to halfway between the island and the farther coast. It apparently does not matter whether the island is just a protruding rock with every third wave washing over the rock. Ownership of that rock can confer title to billions of barrels of oil. You guessed it: several islands stick up in the middle of the South China Sea, and the drilling rights are claimed by six different countries. Although the South China Sea is an attractive prospect, there is little likelihood that it is another Middle East.

Speed Up Exploration

It takes a minimum of 10 years to go from a cold start on a new province to delivery of the first oil. One of the legendary oil finders, Hollis Hedberg, explained it in terms of "the story." When you start out in a new area, you want to know whether the oil is trapped in folds, in reefs, in sand lenses, or along faults. You want to know which are the good reservoir rocks and which are the good cap rocks. The answers to those questions are "the story." After you spend a few years in exploration work and drilling holes, you figure out "the story." For instance, the oil is in fossil patch reefs. Then pow, pow, pow—you bring in discovery after discovery in patch reefs. Even then, there are development wells to drill and pipelines to install. It works, but it takes 10 years. Nothing we initiate now will produce significant oil before the 2004–8 shortage begins.

To summarize: it looks as if an unprecedented crisis is just over the horizon. There will be chaos in the oil industry, in governments, and in national economies. Even if governments and industries were to recognize the problems, it is too late to reverse the trend. Oil production is going to shrink. In an earlier, politically incorrect era the scene would be described as a "Chinese fire drill.". . .

Betting Against Hubbert

What should we do? Doing nothing is essentially betting against Hubbert. Ignoring the problem is equivalent to wagering that world oil production will continue to increase forever. My recommendation is for us to bet that the prediction is roughly correct. Planning for increased energy conservation and designing alternative energy sources should begin now to make good use of the few years before the crisis actually happens.

"Oil is becoming more rather than less plentiful."

Global Oil Reserves Are Not Being Exhausted

Sarah A. Emerson

According to Sarah A. Emerson in the following viewpoint, known oil reserves are growing. In contrast to critics who claim that finite oil reserves will inevitably be exhausted, she contends that oil companies will continue to develop technology that will permit them to locate and extract more oil. Emerson believes that policymakers should recognize the abundance of petroleum resources so that they can make sound energy policies. Sarah A. Emerson is director of Energy Security Analysis, Inc., an energy research firm.

As you read, consider the following questions:
1. According to Emerson, what is Thomas Malthus's theory about resource scarcity?
2. What does Morris Adelman theorize about the quantity of global oil reserves, as related by the author?
3. What are the main factors pushing down the costs of oil exploration, as stated by Emerson?

C oncerns over the "energy security" of an oil-consuming country arise from two commonly held assumptions. The first is the general assumption that global oil supplies are finite and dwindling. The second and more specific assumption is that most of the remaining oil is located in politically unstable regions such as the Middle East. Since the first oil crisis in 1973, these two assumptions have shaped energy policy in the oil-consuming countries of the Organization for Economic Cooperation and Development (OECD). The United States has essentially replaced fuel oil with natural gas in industrial consumption and electric power generation. In Europe, gasoline is so heavily taxed that the price at the pump is as much as five times higher than the price at the refinery gate. European countries have also compelled their refiners and importers to hold a minimum level of petroleum product inventory, while the United States, Japan, Germany, and, more recently, South Korea have built substantial government stockpiles. These and other policies have promoted conservation and now provide a buffer stock that will lessen the short-term price impact of a supply disruption.

Energy Security

Though the issue of energy security remains a perennial concern of oil-importing countries, the global oil market is very different today than it was in the 1970s. Public policy must take into account the fact that the nature of energy security concerns has changed as the motivating assumptions that spawned those concerns have changed. Most importantly, the starting assumption of global resource scarcity is grossly exaggerated in public policy discourse: not only does output from mature producing regions continue to exceed expectations, but the exploration and production frontier continues to expand across countries as geographically and economically disparate as Vietnam, Turkmenistan, Chad, and the United States.

It would be foolhardy to contend that there is enough oil in the ground to meet global demand growth for the next 100 years, but energy policy is not formulated to address 100-year problems. Its horizon can be as near as the next election or as far as the foreseeable future, but even the latter is much closer to 20 years than 100. For any energy security policy to be effective over the next 20 years, it must recognize the resource plenty—as opposed to the resource scarcity—that results from the free flow of capital and technology across an increasingly global resource base. That does not mean that importing countries should ignore the question of energy security, but that policies should go beyond "getting out of oil" or "making the world safe for oil production." Importing countries should consider alternative approaches that encourage safe and efficient development of this abundant resource, especially from regions other than the Middle East. In the process, energy security policy can capitalize on resource plenty and lessen, if not postpone, overwhelming dependence on Middle Eastern oil.

The Theoretical Paradigm

The idea that the world is running out of oil was foreshadowed by Thomas Malthus' contention that the more the world consumes its resources, the less it has left. More recently, in energy circles, the issue has been encapsulated in the concept of "resource scarcity," a term closely associated with Harold Hotelling's 1931 paper, "The Economics of Exhaustible Resources," which has shaped perceptions of oil supply ever since. Hotelling's fundamental argument was that the future price of oil is an inclining curve, largely because the volume of oil in the ground is a finite and fixed stock. Therefore, as each barrel is produced and consumed, remaining barrels become dearer and more expensive.

In the intervening decades, however, Hotelling's premise has been modified if not refuted by subsequent analyses, most notably that of Morris Adelman of the Massachusetts Institute of Technology, who succinctly points out that instead of fixed stocks of resources, there are only flows of reserve-additions. In other words, oil reserves in the ground are not a stock but a flow. On one hand, oil is consumed, which diminishes reserves. On the other hand, the oil industry spends billions of dollars each year exploring for oil and, in the process, adding to reserves. Adelman goes on to say that the industry's objective is to maintain a volume of reserves that is equal to at least 15 years of production, a reserve-to-production ratio of 15. The vast majority of oil producing countries have reserve-to-production ratios far greater than 15, although some of the most mature producing regions, such as the United States and the United Kingdom, have ratios closer to 10.

Phases of Growth in Non-OPEC Supply

Historically, additions to global oil reserves have outpaced production.

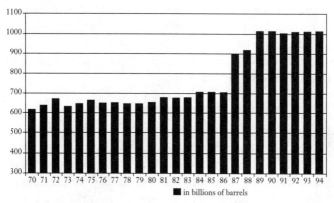

in billions of barrels

BP Statistical Review

According to Adelman, replacement cost is the measure of scarcity. He posits that, "all else being equal, the replacement cost of any mineral should constantly increase over time, and the price with it. First, the average size of new-found deposits should constantly decrease. The biggest would be found first even by chance, let alone by design. Second, the better, (i.e. lower cost) mineral should be used up first." Adelman then responds to his own characterization: "Yet prices of minerals have not risen. Practically all prices have been flat or actually declining in the long run. . . . Mineral depletion is in fact an endless tug of war: diminishing returns versus increasing knowledge. So far, the human race has won big."

That victory is apparent in the historical growth of proven oil reserves. The accompanying graph of reserve estimates since 1970 shows that reserve additions more than offset production almost every year during this 25-year period. This fact alone suggests that oil is becoming more rather than less plentiful. Despite this result, we should put only so much faith in estimates of oil reserves, for the graph also illustrates the political manipulation of official reserve estimates. The hefty 27 percent increase in 1987 followed the 1986 oil price collapse and the end of Saudi Arabia's tenure as swing producer. Most of the increase came in the official reserve estimates for Venezuela, the United Arab Emirates, Iran, and Iraq. All four countries inflated their reserve estimates not only as part of the ensuing battle for market share, but also to position themselves for the subsequent production quota system in which quotas were allocated on the basis of reserve size. The lesson of 1986–1987 is that reserve estimates are not always reliable, but the lesson of the last quarter century is that oil reserves are growing.

The Promise of Technology

Adelman's theory is very compelling. As long as the price of oil exceeds the cost of exploration, development, and extraction, companies will continue to invest in adding to their reserves. The main factors pushing costs down are increases in knowledge and improvements in technology. The resource scarcity argument, therefore, only works if additions to reserves dry up. This will only happen if the industry stops investing, which will only occur if replacement costs exceed price. To believe that replacement costs will exceed price, one must bet against technological innovation. It is the inexorable march of technological development that has allowed the industry to find and produce more and more oil in mature regions at lower and lower cost, while at the same time opening up remote and hostile oil-producing frontiers. The first step in recognizing resource plenty is to abandon Hotelling's fairly simplistic assumption of oil as a fixed stock in favor of Adelman's more subtle characterization of oil reserves as a flow, a flow dependent on continual adaptation and innovation to keep replacement (or production) costs below price. . . .

Resource Plenty as a Foundation for Policy

The concept of resource scarcity is not an appropriate underpinning for energy security policy. Resource plenty, which focuses the policymaker's attention on the future instead of the past, is a much more compelling basis on which to form policy. Given this reorientation in assumptions, policymakers can rank their security concerns and policy responses. If weathering a temporary supply disruption is the objective, then building and maintaining an emergency stockpile is the most direct solution. If the objective is to safeguard the economy against the implied threat of exhausting oil reserves and the resulting price rise, then proper recognition of the implications of resource plenty is essential. The solution is to fashion policy that promotes the efficient and safe development and use of this abundant resource. New technologies in the production and consumption of other energies may one day provide competitive alternatives to oil. Energy policy between now and then should do everything it can to unlock the earth's resource plenty. This is especially true in addressing the concomitant concern that ultimately the oil left will all be in the politically unstable Middle East. The more policy can unshackle the enormous resources in countries outside of the Middle East, the longer ultimate dependence on Middle Eastern oil can be postponed.

"[An] impressive century of growth unfortunately has not translated into adequate food supplies for all the Earth's inhabitants."

Global Food Supplies Are Becoming Scarcer

Lester R. Brown

Lester R. Brown is president of the Worldwatch Institute, a research organization that analyzes and calls attention to global problems. He contends in the following viewpoint that despite significant increases in world food production during the twentieth century, a significant percentage of the world's population suffers from malnutrition. Moreover, the trend of ever-increasing food productivity will likely reverse itself because of global water scarcity, decreasing fish stocks, and depleted rangelands. Brown predicts that impending food shortages will hit those in the developing world hardest, particularly rural people.

As you read, consider the following questions:

1. As cited by Brown, how many people remain hungry and undernourished?
2. Why has China experienced a decrease in the number of malnourished whereas India has seen an increase, in the author's opinion?
3. What does Brown suggest to eliminate world hunger?

Lester R. Brown, "Feeding Nine Billion," *State of the World 1999*, edited by Worldwatch Institute. New York: W.W. Norton, 1999. Copyright © 1999 by Worldwatch Institute. Reproduced by permission.

When the twentieth century began, each American farmer produced enough food to feed seven other people in the United States and abroad. Today, a U.S. farmer feeds 96 people. Staggering gains in agricultural productivity in the United States and elsewhere have underpinned the emergence of the modern world as we know it. Just as the discovery of agriculture itself set the stage for the emergence of early civilization, these gains in agricultural productivity have facilitated the emergence of our modern global civilization.

This has been a revolutionary century for world agriculture. Draft animals have largely been replaced by tractors; traditional varieties of corn, wheat, and rice have given way to high-yielding varieties; and world irrigated area has multiplied sixfold since 1900. The use of chemical fertilizers—virtually unheard of in 1900—now accounts for an estimated 40 percent of world grain production.

Technological advances have tripled the productivity of world cropland during this century. They have helped expand the world grain harvest from less than 400 million tons in 1900 to nearly 1.9 billion tons in 1998. Indeed, farmers have expanded grain production five times as much since 1900 as during the preceding 10,000 years since agriculture began. . . .

Declining Resources

This impressive century of growth unfortunately has not translated into adequate food supplies for all the Earth's inhabitants. An estimated 841 million people remain hungry and undernourished, a number that approaches the population of the entire world when Thomas Malthus warned about the race between food and people some 200 years ago. Unless the world can move quickly to stabilize population, the ranks of the hungry and undernourished could increase as the new millennium unfolds.

Historically, we have depended on three basic systems for our food supply: oceanic fisheries, rangelands, and croplands. With oceanic fisheries and rangelands, two essentially natural systems, the world appears to have "hit the wall." After increasing nearly fivefold since mid-century, the oceanic fish catch appears to be at or near its sustainable yield limit.

Overfishing is now the rule, not the exception. The same can be said about the world's rangelands: after tripling from 1950 to 1990, the production of beef and mutton has increased little in recent years as overgrazing has lowered rangeland productivity in large areas of the world. . . .

The Malnutrition Scourge

The U.N. Food and Agriculture Organization, using national nutritional surveys, estimates that 841 million people living in developing countries suffer from basic protein-energy malnutrition—they do not get enough protein, enough calories, or enough of both. Infants and children lack the food they need to develop their full physical and mental potential. Most of the adults and children in this group do not have the energy to maintain normal levels of physical activity.

As the world has become more economically integrated, the face of famine has changed. Whereas famine was once geographically defined by poor harvests, today it is also economically defined by low productivity and incomes. It is found among those who are on the land but cannot produce enough food or who are in the cities and cannot buy enough. Famine concentrated among the poor is less visible than the more traditional geographically focused version, but it is no less real. Malnutrition weakens the body's immune system to the point where common childhood ailments such as measles and diarrhea are often fatal. Each day 19,000 children die as a result of malnutrition and related illnesses.

The world's hungry children are concentrated in two areas: the Indian subcontinent, where three fifths of all children suffer from malnutrition, and sub-Saharan Africa, where the equivalent figure is 30 percent. Malnutrition among infants and children is of particular concern because anything that stunts their physical development may also stunt their mental development. Malnutrition not only exacts a high social cost, as measured in human suffering, it also depreciates a country's human capital, its most valuable resource.

Many developing countries have socially damaging levels of malnutrition, as measured by the share of children under age five that are underweight. (See Table 1.) Among major countries, Bangladesh and India are at the top of the list.

Other populous countries with a large percentage of underweight children are Viet Nam, Ethiopia, Indonesia, Pakistan, and Nigeria.

Table 1. Share of Children Under Five Years of Age Who Are Underweight in Selected Countries

Country	Share of Underweight (percent)
Bangladesh	66
India	64
Viet Nam	56
Ethiopia	48
Indonesia	40
Pakistan	40
Nigeria	36
Philippines	33
Tanzania	29
Thailand	26
China	21
Zimbabwe	11
Egypt	10
Brazil	7

World Health Organization, *Global Database on Child Growth*, Geneva, 1997, based on national surveys taken between 1987 and 1995.

Over the last half-century, the share of the world that is malnourished has declined substantially. More than anything else, this has been due to rising food production per person. Using grain production per person as the indicator, the world has made substantial progress in raising food consumption since 1950. There has been, however, a loss of momentum since 1984. World grain consumption per person, which averaged 247 kilograms in 1950, had climbed to 342 kilograms by 1984, a gain of 38 percent. During the 14 years since then it has declined to 319 kilograms, a drop of 7 percent. Although there are obvious limitations to using average grain supply as a measure, it is nonetheless much easier in a low-income society to eliminate malnutrition when grain production per person is rising than when it is falling. Since more people are involved in grain production than in any other economic activity in developing countries, a rise in grain output per person means gains in both productivity and consumption.

China and India

This rising global tide of grain production from 1950 to 1984 lifted food consumption for many to a nutritionally adequate level, but the extent of the rise varied widely by country and region of the world. The trends in the two population giants—China and India—that together contain 35 percent of humanity contrast sharply. Although India has made impressive progress in raising grain production, the growth in output has been largely offset by that of population, leaving nearly two thirds of its children malnourished. As a result, the annual grain harvest per person is still slightly less than 200 kilograms per person, providing the average Indian with little more than a starch-dominated subsistence diet. At 200 kilograms, or roughly one pound per day, nearly all grain must be consumed directly just to satisfy basic food energy needs, leaving little to convert into animal protein.

In China, by contrast, the impressive progress in boosting agricultural output after the economic reforms of 1978, combined with a dramatic slowing of population growth, raised grain production per person from roughly 200 to nearly 300 kilograms. This increase, accompanied by record gains in income, let China both raise the amount of grain consumed directly and convert substantial quantities of grain into pork, poultry, and eggs, thus eliminating much of the protein-calorie malnutrition of two decades ago. While the share of underweight children in India remains at 64 percent, that in China had dropped to 21 percent by the late 1980s, when the last nutritional surveys were taken in these two countries. Given the doubling of incomes in China during the 1990s, continuing impressive gains in agriculture, and the latest life expectancy estimate of 71 years, the portion of children malnourished has likely dropped much further. Many of those still malnourished in China live in the interior of the country, often in semiarid regions where rainfall is so low that modern agricultural technologies can make only a modest contribution to raising food output.

Grain consumption per person varies widely by country, providing a rough indicator of nutritional adequacy. The annual consumption figure, including grain consumed indirectly in the form of livestock products, ranges from just under 200 kilograms to more than 900 kilograms. Ironically, the healthiest people in the world are not those at the top of this ladder, but rather those in the middle. Life expectancy in Italy, for example, where on average people get 400 kilograms of grain per year, is higher than in the United States, which uses twice as much grain and has much higher health care expenditures per person. The health of those who live too high on the food chain often suffers from excessive consumption of fat-rich livestock products.

Uneven Distribution

The continued existence of hunger today is largely the result of low productivity, which manifests itself in low incomes and poverty. For the world as a whole, incomes have risen dramatically over the last century, climbing from $1,300 per person in 1900 to more than $6,000 per person in 1998 (in 1997 dollars). This rising economic tide has lifted most of humanity out of poverty and hunger, but unfortunately it has been uneven, leaving many still suffering from poverty and from hunger and malnutrition.

The World Bank estimates that 1.3 billion people live in absolute poverty, with incomes of $1 a day or less. Most of these people live in rural areas. Many try to gain a livelihood from plots of land that have been divided and subdivided as population has increased. Others have too little land to make a living because landownership is concentrated in the hands of a small segment of the population. Still another group consists of rural landless—those who have no land of their own but who work on that of others, often on a seasonal basis. For other individuals, soil erosion and other forms of land degradation are undermining rural livelihoods. Perhaps the fastest growing segment of the absolute poor are those who live in the squatter settlements that ring so many Third World cities.

Consumers the world over have benefited from declining real grain prices over the last half-century, but there is now a possibility that this trend could be reversed as aquifer depletion spreads, shrinking irrigation water supplies. This is particularly important in major countries such as China and India, which rely on irrigated land for half or more of their food and where groundwater depletion will inevitably lead to irrigation cutbacks. There are also scores of smaller countries faced with aquifer depletion, many of them in North Africa and the Middle East, where most of the food comes from irrigated land.

An Ominous Reversal

Fortunately for those on the lower rungs of the global economic ladder, the declining real price of grain created an ideal environment for easing hunger and malnutrition. If this twentieth-century trend of falling grain prices is reversed as we enter the new millennium, as now seems likely, it could impoverish more people in a shorter period of time than any event in history.

If a strategy to eliminate hunger is to succeed, it must simultaneously focus on accelerating the shift to smaller families in order to stabilize population sooner rather than later, raise investment in the rural areas where poverty is concentrated, and design economic policies to distribute wealth more equitably. Any strategy that does not focus on the social investment needs in education and health and in new investments that create productive employment is not likely to accomplish its goal. . . .

A Difficult Challenge

As we prepare for the new millennium, there is a rising tide of concern about the long-term food prospect. This can be seen in the frustration of plant breeders who are running into physiological constraints as they attempt to develop the new higher-yielding varieties needed to restore rapid growth in the world food supply. And it can be seen in the apprehensiveness of political leaders in countries where the food supply depends heavily on irrigation but the aquifers are being depleted. . . .

Adequately feeding the projected increases in population poses one of the most difficult challenges that modern civilization faces.

"On practically every *count, humankind is now* better *nourished."*

Global Food Supplies Are Not Becoming Scarcer

Bjorn Lomborg

Bjorn Lomborg is an associate professor of statistics in the Department of Political Sciences at the University of Aarhus, Denmark. In the following viewpoint, Lomborg asserts that despite enormous population growth, farmers are feeding a higher percentage of people worldwide than ever before. According to Lomborg, the Green Revolution—during which scientists developed fertilizers and pesticides, high-yield crops, and better irrigation methods—enabled farmers to produce more food more cheaply. Inhabitants in both the developed and developing world have benefited as food production has tripled, calorie intake per capita increased, and the number of starving people fallen.

As you read, consider the following questions:

1. Describe Malthus's theory of population growth, as related by the author.
2. According to Lomborg, how much has meat per person increased since 1950?
3. How have Norwegian farmers increased the productivity of salmon, as explained by the author?

"The battle to feed humanity is over. In the course of the 1970s the world will experience starvation of tragic proportions—hundreds of millions of people will starve to death." This was the introduction to one of the most influential books on hunger. Paul Ehrlich's *The Population Bomb* published in 1968. More than 3 million copies of the book have been sold.

Doomsayers Proved Wrong

Ehrlich runs down what he calls the "professional optimists": "They say, for instance, that India in the next eight years can increase its agricultural output to feed some 120 million more people than they cannot after all feed today. To put such fantasy into perspective one need consider only . . .", and Ehrlich presented a whole list of reasons why this could not be achieved. And sure enough, it turned out that the figure of 120 million did not hold water. Eight years later India produced enough food for 144 million more people. And since the population had grown by 'only' 104 million, this meant there was more food to go round.

From the same quarter Lester Brown, who later became president of the Worldwatch Institute, wrote in 1965 that "the food problem emerging in the less-developing regions may be one of the most nearly insoluble problems facing man over the next few decades."

They were both mistaken. Although there are now twice as many of us as there were in 1961, each of us has *more* to eat, in both developed and developing countries. Fewer people are starving. Food is far cheaper these days and food-wise the world is quite simply a better place for far more people.

Malthus and Everlasting Hunger

It seems so obvious, though, that there being more people on the Earth should mean less food for each individual. This simple theory was formulated in 1798 by Reverend Thomas Malthus, an English economist and demographer. The argument was made remarkably popular in the 1970s by the best-seller *Limits to Growth*.

Malthus' theory was that the population grows by a certain percentage a year—i.e. exponentially. The Earth's population currently stands to double in about 40 years. So in 80 years' time there will be four times as many of us and in 120 years eight times as many, etc. Food production grows more slowly—its growth is linear. It may double within 40 years but in 80 years it will only be three times the present level, and in 120 years only four times. The population will grow ever more rapidly while the growth in food supplies will remain constant. So in the long term, food production will lose its race against the population. Many people will starve and die.

Malthus' theory is so simple and attractive that many reputable scientists have fallen for it. But the evidence does not seem to support the theory. The population rarely grows exponentially. Likewise, the quantity of food seldom grows linearly. In actual fact the world's agricultural production has more than doubled since 1961, and in developing countries it has more than tripled. This means that there has been a steady growth in the amount of food available for each member of the population. According to the UN we produce 23 percent more food per capita than we did in 1961, and the growth in agricultural crops per person in developing countries has grown by as much as 52 percent. Equiva-

Figure 1

Daily intake of calories per capita in the industrial and developing countries and world, 1961–1998.

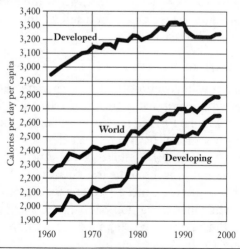

39

Figure 2

Proportion of starving in percent, developing world by region, for 1970, 1980, 1991, 1997, and estimates for 2010.

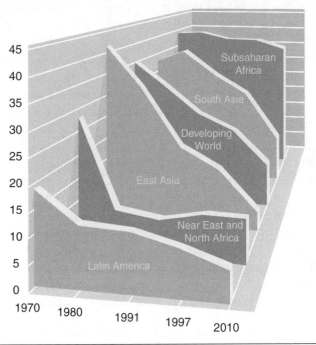

lently, meat per person has grown by 122 percent from 17.2 kg in 1950 to 38.4 kg in 2000. In spite of this dramatic increase in demand the price of food fell by more than two-thirds from 1957 to early 2001.

More Food than Ever

Basically, we now have far more food per person than we used to, even though the population has doubled since 1961. It can be seen from Figure 1 that our calorie intake has increased by 24 percent on a global basis, and that developing countries have experienced a dramatic increase of 38 percent.

The calorie figure is, nonetheless, an average. It is not unthinkable that the figure conceals the fact that some people live better lives while increasing numbers of others just manage or even starve. But here, as elsewhere, things are improving.

According to the UN's definition, a person is starving if

he or she does not get sufficient food to perform light physical activity. Figure 2 shows the percentage of people starving in developing countries. Globally, the proportion of people starving has fallen from 35 percent to 18 percent and is expected to fall further to 12 percent in 2010. This should be compared to an estimated 45 percent of developing country people starving in 1949.

The proportion of children in the developing world considered to be undernourished has fallen from 40 percent to 30 percent over the past 15 years, and it is expected to fall further to 24 percent in 2020. Since 1970, the proportion of starving people has fallen in all regions, and it is set to fall even further for almost all regions.

It is remarkable that the fall in the proportion of people starving in the world should have come at the same time as the population of developing countries doubled. What is more astounding is that the actual *number* of people starving in the Third World has fallen. While in 1971 almost 920 million people were starving, the total fell to below 792 million in 1997. In 2010 it is expected to fall to 680 million. These figures are, of course, still frighteningly high, but it is important to emphasize that today more than 2 billion more people are *not* starving.

The improvement in absolute figures has, however, primarily been in Asia and is largely a consequence of China's amazing ability to produce food.

Lower Prices than Ever

At the same time as the Earth accommodates ever more people, who are making demands for ever more food, food prices have fallen dramatically. In 2000 food cost less than a third of its price in 1957. This fall in food prices has been vital for many people in the developing world, especially the many poverty-stricken city dwellers.

The fall in the price of food is a genuine long-term tendency. The price of wheat has had a downwards trend ever since 1800, and wheat is now more than ten times cheaper than the price charged throughout the previous 500 years. The fall in prices was particularly marked in the post-war period and applied to more or less all major types of food.

The only break in the fall in prices was in the 1970s, when the oil crisis led to heavy price increases in the short term. The increase in the price of oil meant that artificial fertilizers became more expensive and that the Soviet Union, a major oil exporter, was able to buy cereals for its domestic meat production.

Since prices reflect the scarcity of a product, foodstuffs have actually become less scarce during this century despite the fact that the population has more than tripled and demand increased by even more.

The Green Revolution

One cannot help asking oneself how development can possibly have been so good. The answer is to be found in a number of technologies which are collectively known as The Green Revolution.

The Revolution consisted primarily of
- High-yield crops
- Irrigation and controlled water supply
- Fertilizers and pesticides
- Farmers' management skills.

The secret of the Green Revolution was to get more food out of each and every hectare of soil. The vision was that of Norman Borlaug, who later received the Nobel Peace Prize for his work on high-yield varieties of crops. In his laboratories in Mexico attention was focused in particular on the major types of cereals: rice, corn and wheat. Characteristic of these modern varieties is that they germinate earlier in the year, grow faster and are more resistant to disease and drought. They often have shorter stems than the old varieties so that most of the plants' sustenance ends up in the grains.

The fact that the plants germinate earlier and grow more quickly means that in many parts of the world it is possible to harvest two or three crops a year. Rice no longer takes 150 days to mature and many varieties can do so in as little as 90 days. At the same time, it is possible to cultivate crops in large areas where climate conditions are less favorable. For example, modern corn can be grown in an 800 km wider belt around the Earth, which has been a boon to countries like Canada, Russia, China and Argentina. Wheat has become resistant to most diseases, such as mildew and rust, which means a lot in developing countries where farmers often cannot afford pesticides. The new varieties of wheat now account for almost 90 percent of production in developing countries.

Since 1960, the new varieties have led to a 30 percent plus increase in maximum yields and are responsible for 20–50 percent of the total, increased productivity. For farmers in the developing world this also means more money—new varieties are estimated to give farmers an additional income of almost four billion dollars each year.

In fact it is not only varieties of grain that have been improved. Chickens and pigs produce more than twice as much meat as they did 60 years ago and cows produce twice the amount of milk. With genetic enhancement and modern fish farming, the Norwegian salmon has since the early 1970s also become twice as productive.

Irrigation and water control (e.g. building dams) have become more widespread, the proportion of irrigated fields having almost doubled from 10.5 percent in 1961 to over 18 percent in 1997. Irrigation renders the soil far more fertile—it has enabled the Egyptians to get almost twice the wheat yield of the average developing country. Irrigation also makes it possible to harvest two or three times a year. This is why irrigated land contributes as much as 40 percent of the Earth's food—even though it only accounts for 18 percent of the total agricultural land mass. The growth in the use of irrigation has been constant in absolute hectares but is, therefore, slightly declining relatively, partly because of an incipient water scarcity in many regions and partly because of a general fall-off in the demand for food.

Finally, the increased use of fertilizers and pesticides has made it possible to improve plant growth and not lose such a large proportion of crops to disease and insects. Almost a third of the Asian rice harvest was eaten by insects in 1960! The use of fertilizer has increased almost nine-fold since 1950 and although there has been a slight reduction in global consumption because of the Soviet Union's agricultural reforms and later collapse, important countries like China and India still use more fertilizers.

The Green Revolution represents a milestone in the his-

| Figure 3

Yield in tons per hectare of rice, corn and wheat in developing countries, 1960–2000.

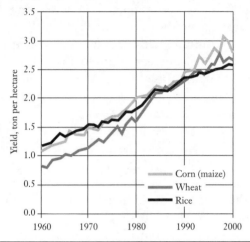

tory of mankind. The ensuing fantastic increase in food production has made it possible to feed far more people. Overall, the Green Revolution has meant a tremendous increase in production per hectare as regards all traditional crops. From Figure 3 it can be seen how the developing countries have experienced an increase in productivity as regards the three most important crops: rice, wheat and corn. Rice production has increased by 122 percent, corn by 159 percent and wheat by a whopping 229 percent. And they still have quite a way to go before they reach the same levels as the industrialized world.

One sometimes hears that the use of pesticides and intensive farming methods are harmful to the environment. But what alternative do we have, with more than 6 billion people on Earth? If we abandoned intensive cultivation and the use of pesticides, farmers would either need *far more space* to grow the same quantities or end up producing *far less food*. So they would either have to take over more of the surrounding countryside or we would end up with more hungry souls among us. . . .

Finally, the new "designer" varieties of crops offer greater resistance to disease, thereby reducing pesticide consumption, while at the same time having improved uptake of nutrients, thus reducing the overapplication of fertilizer. . . .

We Can Feed the World

"The battle to feed mankind is over." The food problem in the developing world represents a "nearly insoluble problem." We have been told for ages that it will end in disaster. That we can't feed the world. But the doomsday vision has nothing to do with reality. On practically *every* count, humankind is now *better* nourished. The Green Revolution has been victorious. Production in the developing countries has tripled. The calorie intake per capita has here increased by 38 percent. The proportion of starving people has fallen from 35 percent to 18 percent and today more than 2 billion more people do not go hungry.

"Twenty thousand square kilometres of Brazil's Amazon rainforest are being destroyed per year, with some years far worse than that."

Rain Forest Destruction Has Reached Crisis Proportions

Peter Bunyard

According to Peter Bunyard in the following viewpoint, claims that the Amazon rain forest is in good health are ignorant and short-sighted. He contends that over twenty thousand square kilometers of Amazonian rain forest are destroyed each year. Because evaporation and transpiration in rain forests fuel the Earth's weather patterns, such widespread damage to the Amazon rain forest could result in climate disruptions worldwide, Bunyard maintains. Peter Bunyard is the science editor of the *Ecologist*, the world's longest-running environmental magazine.

As you read, consider the following questions:

1. As cited by Bunyard, how many square kilometers of Amazonian rain forest were destroyed in 1998?
2. What percentage of the rain that falls in the Amazon rain forest evaporates from the canopy, according to the author?
3. In the author's opinion, what effect will destruction of the Amazon rain forest have on Great Britain?

Peter Bunyard, "Crisis? What Crisis?" *The Ecologist*, vol. 30, October 2000, p. 56. Copyright © 2000 by *The Ecologist*. Reproduced by permission.

According to ex-Greenpeace founding member Patrick Moore, all the stories about the destruction of the Amazon rain forest are 'at best vastly misleading; at worst a gigantic con'. But his facts are plain wrong—the Amazon is still in trouble, and its fate will also affect the planet's climate.

Extravagant Claims

Have you heard the good news? Patrick Moore and professor of biogeography at London University's School of Oriental and African Studies, Philip Stott, have recently gone public with a 'report' in which they insist that the forest is in good health. Only 12.5 percent of the 260 million hectares of forest contained within the 5 million square kilometres of the 'legal' Brazilian Amazon has actually been destroyed, they say. And, furthermore, even that small level of damage has taken 30 years to achieve—so there's plenty left for the fires of the cattle ranchers and the chainsaws of South-Asian logging companies.

Moore has made his name in recent years by turning against the environmental movement which he helped to found. This, it seems, is his latest salvo in his personal crusade to right the wrongs of his past—but it is the most ridiculous yet. In railing against the likes of Sting and today's 'misguided' Greenpeace campaigners (or anyone, for that matter, who has shown concern for rainforest destruction), Moore and Stott have made the extraordinary claim—the keystone of their argument, in fact—that at least half the forest which has been destroyed is in full regeneration and therefore presumably doing its bit as a carbon sink in the battle against carbon emissions and global warming. Their evidence? They have flown all over the Brazilian Amazon and pored over satellite pictures. Furthermore, countless Brazilian officials have told them categorically that tales of wanton destruction are little more than a publicity wheeze by environmentalists to bring the cash rolling in.

Devastating Losses

Stott, as an academic, should know better, and is certainly out of sync with Brazilians and other South Americans who are deeply concerned at the implications of continuing forest destruction. The official figure is that 20,000 square kilometres of Brazil's Amazon rainforest are being destroyed per year, with some years far worse than that, like 1994/95 or 1998 when the figure leapt to nearly 30,000 square kilometres. But those official figures don't take proper account of the growing volume of forest being stripped in the states of Para and Maranhao for charcoal production in pig iron manufacture. In 1990 exports of charcoal-fired pig iron were 260,000 tons.

Seven years later they had topped one million. More than 30 per cent of Maranhao and 15 per cent of Para are now deforested. The state of Rondonia has lost more than a fifth of its forest. The overall figure of 12.5 per cent can lull the ignorant into a false sense of security.

CAN'T SEE THE FOREST FOR THE LUMBER

The Amazon rainforest, spread over the basin's seven million square kilometre area (the United Kingdom [UK] is 35 times smaller) is both a product of and generator of climate. But Moore and Stott think otherwise. Only patches of the forest (biological refugia) were left during the drying out of the last ice-age—therefore, they say, consequently we have more rainforest today than the world had 12,000 years ago.

So that's alright. Yet this unbelievably facile claim displays an ignorance of the vital, contemporary role that the Amazon plays in stabilising global climate.

As Brazilian physicists and climatologists showed long ago, the forests to the west of the Atlantic receive their watering through a chain of evapotranspiration, with the same Atlantic-derived water precipitating as many as seven times as the air currents move from east to west across the Amazon basin. More than 20 per cent of the rain that falls never hits the ground, but is promptly evaporated from the canopy. That is a function of the dense, natural forest. As much as 48 per cent is transpired—again a function of the forest. The Amazon river carries back to the ocean less than half of all the rain that falls. The remainder fuels the stream of massive cumulonimbus clouds that finally send their latent energy into the Hadley Circulation and help spread the energy from the sun to the higher latitudes, to the benefit of all of us in northern Europe.

A few numbers tell us what is actually at stake. The Amazon basin receives 12 million million tonnes of water a year. In energy terms, that amounts to 950 terawatts of latent heat, which is 73 times more energy than that deployed by all humanity across the globe. Just a 20 per cent decline in precipitation and consequently in evapotranspiration will amount to a drastic drop in the energy transported to the higher latitudes, equivalent to at least 15 times the world's use in energy.

We have no idea of the area of Amazon rainforest that must remain intact for the chain of precipitation/evapotranspiration to be sustained. Who knows what the limits are? But even if it were true, there would be nothing reassuring in the claim that 'only 12.5 per cent has gone'. Meanwhile, the prediction from the UK Met Office that global warming could [destroy] the Amazon rainforest within 50 years, quite apart from the current destruction, is deeply alarming. If the Gulf Stream falters because of global warming and the Amazon rainforest has gone, then we can surely expect a serious chill up in this region of the world [Great Britain].

But then, if Stott and Moore are right, what has the Amazon got to do with us in Britain? According to them it's not something we should be worrying our silly little heads about.

"The [Amazon rain] forest is nearly 90 percent intact."

The Extent of Rain Forest Destruction Has Been Exaggerated

Marc Morano and Kent Washburn

Marc Morano and Kent Washburn contend in the following viewpoint that environmentalists and celebrities have wildly exaggerated the extent of the destruction of the Amazon rain forest. According to Morano and Washburn, only 12.5 percent of the Amazon has been deforested, and of that, one-half is fallow or in the process of regeneration. In fact, studies have shown that trees grow back in commercially logged forests, the authors assert. Marc Morano, a correspondent for *American Investigator*, a television newsmagazine, coproduced with Kent Washburn the documentary *Amazon Rainforest: Clearcutting the Myths*.

As you read, consider the following questions:

1. What environmental groups are conducting "Save the Rain Forest" campaigns, according to Morano and Washburn?
2. As cited by the authors, how long have rain forests existed on Earth?
3. How did the Mayans interact with the Amazon rain forest, as related by Morano and Washburn?

P atrick Moore became an instant celebrity in 1977 when a photograph showing him cradling a baby seal in defiance of arrest by Canadian authorities was broadcast around the world.

As the front man for the environmental activist group Greenpeace, he helped turn public opinion around on the high-profile issues of whaling, seal hunting, nuclear power and chemical pollution.

Rainforest Myths

Today the environmental scientist and leader of a group called Greenspirit has a new cause—alerting the public to what he calls the "myth" that the Amazon rainforest is endangered by development and deforestation.

"The Amazon is actually the least endangered forest in the world," states Moore in American Investigator's television newsmagazine documentary, "Clear-cutting the myths," hosted by former CBS and CNN newsman Reid Collins. Moore explains that, in the 20 years of warnings about deforestation, "only 10 percent of the Amazon has been converted to date from what was original forest to agriculture and settlement."

The finding that the Amazon rainforest threat is a myth based on bad science and political agendas—especially by unlikely critics such as Moore, other scientists and inhabitants of the region—is not expected to sit well with a movement that has enlisted schoolchildren throughout the United States and celebrities ranging from Sting to Alec Baldwin to Chevy Chase to Tom Jones and Tony Bennett. And which has also raised tens of millions of dollars for environmental activist groups.

"This is where I really have a problem with modern-day environmentalism," says Moore. "It confuses opinion with what we know to be true, and disguises what are really political agendas with environmental rhetoric. The fact of the matter is: There is a larger percentage of the Amazon rain forest intact than there are most other forests in this world."

Moore left Greenpeace, the organization he helped found, in 1986, after finding himself at odds with other leaders of the group.

"We had already helped the world turn the corner on the environmental issues," he said. "Once a majority agrees with you, its time to stop beating them over the head and sit down with them and try to figure out some solutions."

Popular Culture Mythologizing

Yet, the notion that the Amazon jungles are threatened remains embedded in the popular culture:

The 1993 animated feature, "Ferngully: The Last Rainforest," takes the Amazon's mystical charm literally, showing magical rainforest fairies fighting for their lives against industrialist's chainsaws and bulldozers.

National Geographic's "Rainforest: Heroes of the High Frontier" warns that "despite efforts to save it, the rainforest is being consumed at an unprecedented rate."

"Amazonia: A Celebration of Life" shows playful jungle animals being rudely awakened to the sound of chainsaws.

The 1992 Sean Connery feature "Medicine Man" shows Connery discovering the cure for cancer at his makeshift lab in the heart of a burning Amazon rainforest. He loses the cure when developers raze his facility in order to build a road.

Environmental groups from Greenpeace to the Sierra Club to the World Wilderness Foundation to the Environmental Defense Fund to the Smithsonian Institution conduct outreach efforts in the name of the rainforest. Dozens of other groups with names like Rainforest Relief, Rainforest Action Network and Rainforest Foundation were created for the sole purpose of exploiting the issue.

A tourist to Brazil who picks up a "Lonely Planet" travel book will read numerous pleas for help: "Unless things change . . . Indians will die with their forests," it pleads. "Invaluable, irreplaceable Amazon may be lost forever."

"Lonely Planet" has company on the bookshelf: "At the current rate of deforestation," [former] Vice President Al Gore writes in "Earth in the Balance," "Virtually all of the world's tropical rainforests will be gone partway though the next century."

The scientific evidence paints a much brighter picture of deforestation in the Amazon. Looking at the NASA Landsat satellite images of the deforestation rates in the Amazon rainforest, about 12.5 percent has been cleared. Of the 12.5 percent, one half to one third of that is fallow, or in the process of regeneration, meaning that at any given moment up to 94 percent of the Amazon is left to nature. Even the Environmental Defense Fund and Sting's Rainforest Foundation concede, among the fine print, that the forest is nearly 90 percent intact.

The Forest Dwellers' Perspective

Fabio Ferreira, a Cabloco, or [Amazon] forest dweller, said, "These [environmental] groups do not have a right to tell us what to do, because it is a matter of survival." Cablocos have traditionally relied on subsistence farming, but in recent years food has become more scarce, as environmental regulations have severely limited their ability to use land. Chief Samuel of the Terra Preta explained that he was less concerned about keeping the Amazon totally undisturbed. Instead, his concerns were rather more parochial: "Number one is, how do we survive? We would like more progress."

Allison Freeman, *CEI Updates*, August 31, 2000.

Philip Stott of the University of London and author of the new book, "Tropical Rainforests: Political and Hegemonic Myth-making," maintains that the environmental campaigns have lost perspective.

"One of the simple, but very important, facts is that the rainforests have only been around for between 12,000 and 16,000 years," he says. "That sounds like a very long time, but in terms of the history of the earth, it's hardly a pinprick. The simple point is that there are now still—despite what humans have done—more rainforests today than there were 12,000 years ago."

Moore maintains that "the rainforests of the Amazon, the Congo, Malaysia, Indonesia and a few other parts of the world are the least endangered forests" because "they are the least suitable for human habitation."

Football Fields

Despite the Amazon being at least 87.5 percent intact, many claims abound as to how fast the forest is being cleared.

In "Amazonia," the narrator intones that "in the brief amount of time it takes to watch this film, roughly 400,000 acres of forest will have been cleared." Ruy de Goes of Greenpeace Brazil says in the last four years "an area the size of France was destroyed."

Actor William Shatner in a National Geographic documentary claims that worldwide, "Rainforest is being cleared at a rate of 20 football fields a minute." Rainforest Action Network says the Amazon is being deforested at a rate of eight football fields a minute. Tim Keating of Rainforest Relief says that the deforestation can be measured in seconds. "It may be closer to two to three football fields a second," says Keating.

When de Goes of Greenpeace Brazil is confronted with the disparity in numbers regarding these football fields, he replies, "The numbers are not important, what is important is that there is huge destruction going on."

However, Moore says that the only way such huge numbers are generated is by using double accounting. "You would have cleared 50 times the size of the Amazon already if accurate."

Luis Almir, of the state of Amazonas in Brazil calculated using five football fields a minute and concludes sarcastically that if the numbers were correct, "we would have a desert bigger than the Sahara."

A Blip to the System

Another familiar claim of the environmentalist community is that the Amazon constitutes the "lungs of the earth," supplying one-fifth of the world's oxygen. But, according to Antonio Donato Nobre . . . and other eco-scientists, the Amazon consumes as much oxygen as it produces, and Stott says it may actually be a net user of oxygen.

"In fact, because the trees fall down and decay, rainforests actually take in slightly more oxygen than they give out," says Stott. "The idea of them soaking up carbon dioxide and giving out oxygen is a myth. It's only fast-growing young trees that actually take up carbon dioxide."

Stott maintains that the tropical forests of the world are "basically irrelevant" when it comes to regulating or influencing global weather. He explains that the oceans have a much greater impact.

"Most things that happen on land are mere blips to the system, basically insignificant," he says. . . .

Reversible Damage

The idea that a cleared rainforest can grow back is an idea that is not accepted by most environmental campaigns and the popular culture.

Yet recent studies indicate that trees do in fact regrow very well in rainforests. A 1998 study by Charles Cannon of Duke University found that eight years after industrial logging in Indonesian rainforests, recovery of both native flora and fauna far exceeded expectations. In Borneo, logged forest contained just as many tree species as unlogged forest.

"These findings warrant reassessment of the conservation potential of large tracts of commercially logged tropical rainforest," wrote Cannon.

Science magazine contributor Robin Chazdon, an ecologist at the University of Connecticut, says: "You can find species that will show increased growth and increased population as a result of logging.". . .

A Long History

Despite all of this mounting scientific evidence supporting regeneration, many still want to keep mankind out of the Amazon and other tropical forests. Chazdon believes that it is not very realistic to keep man out.

"No matter how hard we try," she says, "it's hard to put a lock and key on the forests." She points out that great civilizations once inhabited Central and South America and newly discovered charcoal deposits and agricultural artifacts suggest that humans have repeatedly burned the rainforest. "We are part of the long history of humans that have relied on these forests and used them," pointing out that "the Mayan Empire deforested huge areas of Central America."

Periodical Bibliography

The following articles have been selected to supplement the diverse views presented in this chapter.

John Bacher	"Petrotyranny," *Earth Island Journal*, Spring 2002.
Peter Bunyard	"Eradicating the Amazon Rainforest Will Wreak Havoc on the Climate, *Ecologist*, March/April 1999.
Charles H. Cannon	"Tree Species Diversity in Commercially Logged Bornean Rainforest," *Science*, August 28, 1998.
Thomas J. Donohue	"World Hunger," *Vital Speeches*, December 1, 1999.
Jefferson G. Edgens	"The Myth of Farmland Loss," *Forum for Applied Research and Public Policy*, Fall 1999.
Wayne Ellwood	"Mired in Crude," *New Internationalist*, June 2001.
High Iltis	"Extinction Is Forever," *Resurgence*, November/December 1997.
Richard A. Kerr	"USGS Optimistic on World Oil Prospects," *Science*, July 14, 2000.
George McGovern	"The Real Cost of Hunger," *UN Chronicle*, September/November 2001.
Patrick Moore	"Brazil of the North," www.greenspirit.com.
Per Pinstrup-Anderson	"Feeding the World in the New Millennium: Issues for the New U.S. Administration," *Environment*, July 2001.
James Riggle	"Farmland Everywhere," *CEI Update*, January 1998.
Peter Rosset, Joseph Collins, and Frances Moore Lappe	"Lessons from the Green Revolution," *Tikkun*, March 2000.
James Srodes	"No Oil Painting," *Spectator*, August 29, 1998.
Bob Wildfong	"Saving Seeds," *Alternatives Journal*, Winter 1999.

CHAPTER 2

What Agricultural Policies Should Be Pursued?

Chapter Preface

Until about four decades ago, the world's crops were grown on family farms. A typical farmer grew several crops, which he rotated on an annual basis. For example, a corn farmer grew corn along with several other food crops such as soybeans as well as the clovers, alfalfa, and small grains that he could feed to livestock. The rotation of several types of crops was the key to the health of the farm. Since different plants use different nutrients in the soil, the farmer could ensure that the soil was not depleted of any one nutrient by rotating. Crop rotation also helped keep pests to a minimum, since growing different plants in different years broke the lifecycles of the pests that fed on them.

However, in the 1950s, these traditional farming methods began to change. The "Green Revolution" ushered in new agricultural methods that transformed food production in the Western world. The single most important change was the shift from crop rotation to monocultures, where the same crop (usually corn, wheat, or rice) is grown each year in the same field. Farmers began to specialize in one or two genetically uniform crops, which produced greater yields than traditionally grown crops. Farmers also began to invest in increasingly sophisticated machinery that enabled them to harvest crops more efficiently. Pesticides and herbicides were developed to help farmers control the pests that proliferated with the end of crop rotation, and synthetic fertilizers were applied to quickly depleted soils. As the Green Revolution progressed, small family farms eventually gave way to factory farms, which were owned by corporations. Agribusiness—as, collectively, factory farms are called—has become the center of intense controversy.

Miguel A. Altieri, associate professor of Agroecology at the University of California at Berkeley, claims that "excessive reliance on farm specialization (including crop monocultures) and inputs such as capital-intensive technology, pesticides, and synthetic fertilizers, has negatively impacted the environment." He argues that the intensification of food production has led to soil erosion, loss of soil productivity, and the depletion of nutrient reserves. Intensive use of pesticides has polluted groundwater and actually increased the number of pests by eliminating their natural enemies, he claims. Many analysts contend that the increase in food yields as a result of specialization is more than offset by increased crop losses due to pests.

Concern about modern agricultural methods has led to calls for "sustainable agriculture," farming practices that promote strong food yields without harming the environment. Sustainable agriculture would rely less heavily on pesticides and fertilizers and would return to some form of crop rotation. However, agribusiness proponents contend that a move to sustainable agriculture would result in a worldwide decrease in food production at a time when there are more human mouths to feed than ever. To revert to past practices, they say, would endanger the lives of countless millions. Factory farm advocates argue that a return to more traditional agricultural methods, such as organic farming, would harm the environment as well. Since organic farms produce lower field yields per acre, more wild lands would have to be converted to cropland, they claim. Dennis T. Avery, director of the Center for Global Food Issues, maintains that "if the world does not triple the yields on the high-quality land currently in farming, we will pay the price . . . in forests and wild meadows cleared to produce more meat, milk, and produce."

The Green Revolution has produced spectacular gains in food production while at the same time generated serious concern about environmental degradation. In the following chapter, authors debate what agricultural methods should be pursued. Debates about how best to grow food will assuredly become more vociferous as the human population grows.

"In the future, [genetically modified foods] could fill the world's larders with high-protein cereals, vegetables with extra vitamins, and all manner of cheaper, tastier and more nutritious foods."

Genetically Engineered Foods Should Be Produced

Economist

In the following viewpoint, the *Economist* argues that genetically modified organisms (GMOs) could prevent a global food crisis caused by human population growth. The magazine claims that scientists have already produced GMOs that are more resistant to insects and more tolerant of herbicides, and they may succeed in developing GMOs that would be more nutritious than non-modified foods. Despite their promise, GMOs have come under attack by wealthy nations at the detriment of nations struggling to feed their people, the *Economist* claims. The *Economist* is a weekly magazine on political and economic issues.

As you read, consider the following questions:
1. According to the *Economist*, what was the "Green Revolution"?
2. What unforeseen health risk is associated with the soyabean which has Brazil nut genes, as stated by the magazine?
3. As defined by the *Economist*, what is Bt cotton?

S hrimps are messy creatures. When scrubbed, shelled and served with lime leaves and lemon grass in a hot Thai tom yam koong soup, they taste wonderful. But while alive, they excrete large amounts of toxic sludge.

On Thai shrimp farms, the traditional way of dealing with this sludge is to toss it in the nearest river. Land used for shrimp farming soon becomes polluted and unusable, so shrimp farmers keep cutting down fresh forest to build new shrimp pools. Since farmed shrimps live in their own waste, they often fall sick. So farmers stuff them with antibiotics, which could end up in your tom yam koong.

Fortunately, there is a technological fix. Bio Solutions, a Thai firm, has developed a pill containing bacteria that eat shrimp excrement. Throw the pill in the pool, and the bacteria multiply until they run out of food. Then they obligingly starve to death, in a tidy, biodegradable way. "If Asia is going to feed itself," says Charles Liu, the president of Bio Solutions, "agricultural biotechnology has to be part of the answer." That is what you would expect him to say—but he has a point.

The Green Revolution

Predictions that people would multiply beyond their capacity to feed themselves, like those Thai bacteria, have repeatedly been proved wrong. In 1798, Thomas Malthus foretold famine just as farm yields were taking off. To his credit, he later admitted that he was wrong. Not so Paul Ehrlich, an American biologist who wrote in 1969: "The battle to feed humanity is over. In the 1970s hundreds of millions of people will starve to death." They didn't.

The world's population grew much as expected, but food output more than kept pace. During the 1960s and 70s, a "green revolution" swept the developing world. Millions of farmers started using higher-yielding hybrid seeds, chemical fertilisers, pesticides and weed-killers. The results were remarkable. For example, Mr Ehrlich had predicted that by the mid-1970s, India would be so obviously beyond hope that America would stop sending food aid. Yet by 1990, India was exporting surplus grain. Chinese rice farmers, using similar techniques, raised production by two-thirds between

1970 and 1995. By one estimate, the green revolution saved a billion people from starvation.

There were some side-effects. Governments subsidised the new chemicals, which encouraged their over-use. This damaged the environment in many parts of the developing world. But the main worry about the green revolution is that it has run out of steam. There are still areas—mainly in Africa—where its techniques have yet to be tried. But in most of the developing world, the gains in productivity from it are tailing off.

Improving Productivity

Globally, 800m people are still malnourished. Heavily subsidised farmers in rich countries produce enough surplus food to feed the hungry, but not at a price the hungry can afford. Even if the rich world's surplus were simply given to the poor, this would not solve the problem. Most poor people earn their living from agriculture, so a deluge of free food would destroy their livelihoods. The only answer to world hunger is to improve the productivity of farmers in poor countries.

This will be difficult. The developing world's population is growing fast, but the amount of land available for cultivation is not. To feed the 2 billion new mouths expected by 2025, new ways must be found to squeeze more calories out of each hectare. But then more people means not just more stomachs to fill, but also more brains to figure out how to fill them.

There are plenty of good ideas available. The most powerful is biotechnology, and especially genetic modification (GM). It is a young science: biologists first found ways of manipulating recombinant DNA in the early 1970s. The first commercially available genetically modified organism (GMO) appeared a mere five years ago. Supporters of GM expect it to end world hunger. Opponents fear it may poison us all. It is worth stepping back for a moment to consider the evidence.

For and Against GMOs

Farmers have been manipulating genomes since long before they knew about genes. For thousands of years, they sought to transfer desirable traits from one plant species to another by cross-breeding: this was how wild grasses were turned into wheat. They also selectively bred animals to make them fatter and tastier: this was how wild boars became pigs.

GM aims to achieve similar results, but faster. It typically takes 8–12 years to produce a better plant by cross-breeding. But if scientists can isolate a gene in one species that is associated with, say, the ability to grow in salty soil, they can sometimes transfer it directly into the genetic code of another species, without spending years crossing successive generations.

GM is more precise than cross-breeding, too. As any parent knows, sexual reproduction is unpredictable. The union of a brilliant woman and an athletic man does not always produce a brilliant and athletic child. In plants, as in people, some traits are inherited, others are not. At least in theory, GM solves this problem by transferring only the gene associated with the trait that the farmer wants.

The final advantage of GM is that it allows the transfer of traits between unrelated species. You cannot cross-breed cacti with corn, but you can take a cactus gene that promotes drought resistance and put it in a corn plant.

So far, scientists have produced GM crops that are more resistant to viruses and insects, and more tolerant of herbicides. In the future, GM could fill the world's larders with high-protein cereals, vegetables with extra vitamins, and all manner of cheaper, tastier and more nutritious foods than we currently enjoy. Researchers at Cornell University in America have even created bananas that contain a vaccine for hepatitis B. A single banana chip inoculates a child for one-fifteenth of the price of an injection, and with fewer tears.

Potential Dangers

Against these actual and potential benefits must be set the potential dangers. Shifting genes between different species could create health risks. For example, soyabeans given brazil nut genes have bean found to express brazil nut proteins of the sort that might trigger allergic reactions. Soyabeans are used in thousands of food products, so if the problem had not been spotted this could have made life hazardous for people with nut allergies.

GM crops may also cause environmental problems. Their

pollen might blow into fields of ordinary crops and fertilise them. There is no evidence that this has happened so far, but it is possible, with unknown effects. Also, crops genetically modified to repel pests might spur the evolution of super-pests or poison other species. Laboratory tests have shown that butterfly larvae are harmed when fed the pollen of plants genetically modified to express a toxin called Bacillus thuringiensis (Bt), which protects corn from corn borers and cotton from boll worms.

All these risks are rather speculative. As with any new technology, it is impossible ever to prove conclusively that GM foods are safe. It is essential to test GM products care-fully before releasing them, and to keep monitoring them af-terwards. But so far, there is no evidence that GM crops hurt either humans or the environment. Americans have been munching modified corn and soyabeans for six years without discernible harm. And so far it looks as though GM crops ac-tually help protect the environment, by reducing the need for chemical pesticides.

GM Crops in the Developing World

Last year, about 44m hectares of transgenic crops were planted, more than 20 times the area in 1996. Most of these fields, however, were in North America. Developing coun-tries have yet to see much benefit from GM technology. But that could change. Among poor countries, the most enthu-siastic adopter of GM technology has been China, where the government frets about food security. In 1997–99, China gave 26 commercial approvals for GM crops, including transgenic peppers, tomatoes, rice and cotton. The most commercially successful of these has been Bt cotton.

Cotton-chomping boll worms have grown resistant to pesticides. In 1992, these worms destroyed the entire cotton crop in some parts of China, ruining large numbers of farm-ers and bankrupting textile factories. So when Monsanto, a big American biotech firm, started selling boll-worm-resistant Bt cotton seeds, the Chinese government snapped them up. Bt cotton now covers half a million hectares of Chinese soil. Production costs have fallen by 14%, despite the hefty price that Monsanto charges for its seeds. Chinese scientists are now working on their own GMOs, and have already produced at least four new versions of Bt cotton.

Dissident Voices

The Chinese example is hopeful, but not unambiguously so. One reason that China's government was able to embrace GM technology is that the country is a dictatorship. Dissident voices are silenced or ignored. A few democracies, such as America, Canada and Argentina, have taken to GM food. But in Europe, although regulators say that GM products are safe, an energetic campaign by non-governmental organisations (NGOs) has convinced consumers that they are not, and dissuaded supermarkets from stocking them. Through the Internet, the campaign has spread to the developing world.

Benson. © 1999 by *Arizona Republic*. Reprinted by permission of the United Feature Syndicate.

India, like China, has lots of poor rural folk who must somehow be fed. Anything that raises rural incomes is likely to help. Indian field trials found that Bt cotton produced 40% more fibre than ordinary cotton, with five fewer chemical sprays for each crop. For a typical small farmer with five hectares, this would save $50 per season, a huge sum by local standards. The farmer would also inhale less pesticide. Despite these findings, the Indian government refuses to permit the commercial planting of Bt cotton, largely because of pressure from NGOs. Protesters have invaded field trials and burned GM crops. Some even blocked the delivery of American food aid to cyclone victims, arguing that it probably contained GM products.

Some poor countries hesitate to plant GMOs for fear of upsetting Europeans. NGOs claim that GM crops may "contaminate" neighbouring fields with their pollen. It would be a short step to call for a boycott of all the food exports, modified and unmodified, of countries where GMOs are widely grown. Even for developing countries that allow GM crops to be planted only in isolated plots for research purposes, the risk of a boycott remains. The peasants who live near research centres often notice how good the new crops are and steal the seeds.

Unlike the techniques of the green revolution, GM technology was largely developed by private companies. In the eyes of many, this made it suspect, but such suspicion is largely misplaced. The profit motive gives companies a strong incentive not to poison their customers. But it gives them no incentive to cater for people who cannot afford their products. Better versions of poor people's staples, such as millet, sorghum and cassava, will probably appear only if governments pay for some of the research, but the current hysteria about GMOs makes this politically difficult. When the United Nations Development Program (UNDP) recently suggested that GM technology could help the poor, it was met with howls of outrage.

The Many Ways of Fighting Hunger

GM is not the only weapon in the war on hunger. Democracy is important too: famines usually occur only in dictatorships. And other technologies too can produce impressive results: using less controversial biotechnology, the UNDP and the Japanese government recently produced a high-yielding hybrid rice that grows faster and contains more protein than ordinary varieties. But battles are easier to win if you have many weapons at your disposal. To remove the most powerful one from the arsenal seems unwise.

For the poor, GM appeared at an awkward time. After several people in Britain died of what was almost certainly a human version of mad-cow disease, Europeans lost faith in their governments' ability to keep dangerous food off their plates. Since people in rich countries rarely go hungry, they were not wildly excited about the promise of cheap and abundant food. Perhaps they will change their minds when scientists create better rather than simply cheaper foods: cholesterol-free bacon, perhaps. But in the meantime, it is sad that the priorities of the well-fed few should make it harder for the world's hungry billions to feed themselves.

"The tools of genetic engineering . . . steal nature's harvest by destroying biodiversity, increasing the use of herbicides and pesticides, and spreading the risk of irreversible genetic pollution."

Genetically Engineered Foods Should Not Be Produced

Vandana Shiva

Vandana Shiva contends in the following viewpoint that genetic engineering will not enhance global food security. On the contrary, according to Shiva, genetically modified organisms (GMOs) will lead to the development of chemical-resistant insects and weeds that could quickly destroy global crops. In addition, she argues that GMOs actually have lower food yields than non-modified crops. Vandana Shiva is the director of the Research Foundation for Science, Technology, and Natural Resource Policy and author of several books, including *Biopiracy: The Plunder of Nature* and *Knowledge and Monocultures of the Mind.*

As you read, consider the following questions:
1. As stated by the author, what are "superweeds"?
2. What are Bt-crops, as defined by Shiva?
3. According to a 1998 study cited by the author, how much lower were the yields of Roundup Ready soybeans compared to the yields of top conventional varieties?

Vandana Shiva, *Stolen Harvest: The Hijacking of the Global Food Supply.* Cambridge, MA: South End Press, 2000. Copyright © 2000 by Vandana Shiva. Reproduced by permission of the publisher.

Genetic engineering has been sold as a green technology that will protect nature and biodiversity. However, the tools of genetic engineering are designed to steal nature's harvest by destroying biodiversity, increasing the use of herbicides and pesticides, and spreading the risk of irreversible genetic pollution.

According to the president of Monsanto, Hendrik Verfaillie, all biodiverse species that are not patented and owned by them are weeds that "steal the sunshine." Yet corporations that promote genetic engineering steal nature's harvest of diverse species, either by deliberately destroying biodiversity or by unintended biological pollution of species and ecosystems. They steal the global harvest of healthy and nutritious food. Finally, they steal knowledge from citizens by stifling independent science and denying consumers the right to know what is in their food. . . .

The Myth of Safe Foods

Monsanto and other corporations repeatedly refer to their seeds and foods as having been tested for safety. But not only have no ecological or food-safety tests been conducted on genetically engineered crops and foods before commercialization; corporations have tried every means within their reach to steal the right to safe and nutritious food from citizens and consumers.

It is often claimed that there have been no adverse consequences from over 500 field releases in the United States. In 1993, for the first time, the data from the U.S. Department of Agriculture (USDA) field trials were evaluated to see whether they support these safety claims. The Union of Concerned Scientists (UCS), which conducted the evaluation, found that the data collected by the USDA on small-scale tests have little value for commercial risk-assessment. Many reports fail to even mention—much less measure—environmental risks. Of those reports that allude to environmental risk, most have only visually scanned field plots looking for stray plants or isolated test crops from relatives. The UCS concluded that the observations that "nothing happened" in those hundreds of tests do not say much. In many cases, adverse impacts are subtle and would never be registered by scanning a field. In other cases, failure to observe evidence of the risk is due to the contained conditions of the tests. Many test crops are routinely isolated from wild relatives, a situation that guarantees no out-crossing. The UCS cautioned that "care should be taken in citing the field test record as strong evidence for the safety of genetically engineered crops."

All genetically engineered crops use genes that are resistant to antibiotics to help identify whether the genes that have been introduced from other organisms have been successfully inserted into the engineered crop. These marker genes can exacerbate the spread of antibiotic resistance among humans. Based on this concern, Britain rejected Ciba-Geigy's transgenic maize, which contains the weaker gene for campicillin resistance.

Many transgenic plants are engineered for resistance to viral diseases by incorporating the gene for the virus's coat protein. These viral genes may cause new diseases. New broad-range recombinant viruses could arise, causing major epidemics.

Upon consumption, the genetically engineered DNA of these foods can break down and enter the blood stream. It has long been assumed that the human gut is full of enzymes that can rapidly digest DNA. But in a study designed to test the survival of viral DNA in the gut, mice were fed DNA from a bacterial virus, and large fragments were found to survive passage through the gut and to enter the bloodstream. Further studies indicate that the ingested DNA can end up in the spleen and liver cells as well as in white blood cells.

Within the gut, vectors carrying antibiotic-resistance markers may also be taken up by the gut bacteria, which would then serve as a mobile reservoir of antibiotic-resistance genes for pathogenic bacteria. Horizontal gene transfer between gut bacteria has already been demonstrated in mice and chickens and in human beings.

When L-tryptophan, a nutritional supplement, was genetically engineered and first marketed, 37 people died and 1,500 people were severely affected by a painful and debilitating circulatory disorder called eosinophilia myalgia. When a gene from the Brazil nut was inserted into soybeans to increase their protein levels, the transgenic soybeans also contained the nut's allergenic properties.

Greenpeace and other non-governmental organizations have revealed that soybean plants sprayed with Roundup are more estrogenic and could act as hormone or endocrine-system disrupters. Dairy cows that consume Roundup Ready soybeans produce milk with higher fat levels than cows that eat regular soybeans.

The Myth of Food Security

The Green Revolution narrowed the basis of food security by displacing diverse nutritious food grains and spreading monocultures of rice, wheat, and maize. However, the Green Revolution focused on staple foods and their yields. The genetic engineering revolution is undoing the narrow gains of the Green Revolution both by neglecting the diversity of staples and by focusing on herbicide resistance, not higher yields.

According to Clive James, transgenic crops are not engineered for higher yields. Fifty-four percent of the increase in transgenic crops is for those engineered for herbicide resistance, or, rather, the increased use of herbicides, not increased food. As an industry briefing paper states, "The herbicide tolerant gene has no effect on yield per se." Worldwide, 40 percent of the land under cultivation by genetically engineered crops is under soybean cultivation, 25 percent under corn, 13 percent under tobacco, 11 percent under cotton, 10 percent under canola, and 1 percent each under tomato and potato. Tobacco and cotton are non-food commercial crops, and crops such as soybeans have not been food staples for most cultures outside East Asia. Such crops will not feed the hungry. Soybeans will not provide food security for *dal*-eating Indians, and corn will not provide security in the sorghum belt of Africa.

The trend toward the cultivation of genetically engineered crops indicates a clear narrowing of the genetic basis of our food supply. Currently, there are only two commercialized staple-food crops. In place of hundreds of legumes and beans eaten around the world, there is soybean. In place of diverse varieties of millets, wheats, and rices, there is only corn. In place of the diversity of oil seeds, there is only canola.

These crops are based on expanding monocultures of the same variety engineered for a single function. In 1996, 1.9 million acres around the world were planted with only two varieties of transgenic cotton, and 1.3 million acres were planted with Roundup Ready soybeans. As the biotechnology industry globalizes, these monoculture tendencies will increase, thus further displacing agricultural biodiversity and creating ecological vulnerability.

Further, by forcing the expansion of non-food crops such as tobacco and cotton, transgenic crops result in fewer acres in food production, aggravating food insecurity.

The Destruction of Biodiversity

In Indian agriculture, women use up to 150 different species of plants (which the biotech industry would call weeds) as medicine, food, or fodder. For the poorest, this biodiversity is the most important resource for survival. In West Bengal, 124 "weed" species collected from rice fields have economic importance for local farmers. In a Tanzanian village, over 80 percent of the vegetable dishes are prepared from uncultivated plants. Herbicides such as Roundup and the transgenic crops engineered to withstand them therefore destroy the economies of the poorest, especially women. What is a weed for Monsanto is a medicinal plant or food for rural people.

Since biodiversity and polycultures are an important source of food for the rural poor, and since polycultures are the most effective means of soil conservation, water conservation, and ecological pest and weed control, the Roundup Ready technologies are in fact a direct assault on food security and ecological security.

The Risks of Genetic Pollution

Genetically engineered crops increase chemical use and add new risks of genetic pollution. Herbicide-resistant crops are designed for intensive use of herbicides in agriculture. But they also create the risks of weeds being transformed into "superweeds" by the transfer of herbicide-resistant traits from the genetically engineered crops to closely related plants.

Research in Denmark has shown that oilseed rape genetically engineered to be herbicide-tolerant could transmit its introduced gene to a weedy natural relative through hybridization. Weedy relatives of rape are now common in Denmark and throughout the world. Converting these "weeds" into "superweeds" that carry the gene for herbicide-resistance would provoke high crop losses and increasing use of herbicides. For these reasons, the European Union has imposed a *de facto* moratorium on the commercial planting of genetically engineered crops.

Wright. © 1999 by *Palm Beach Post*. Reprinted by permission of Tribune Media Services.

In many cases, the weeds that plague cultivated crops are relatives of the crops themselves. Wild beets have been a major problem in European sugar-beet cultivation since the 1970s. Given the gene exchange between weedy beets and cultivated beets, herbicide-resistant sugar beets could only be a temporary solution.

Superweeds could lead to "bioinvasions," displacing local diversity and taking over entire ecosystems. The problem of invasive species is being increasingly recognized as a major threat to biodiversity. Monsanto's claim that products such as Roundup Ready soybeans will reduce herbicide use is false because it does not take into account the introduction of such engineered plants in regions where herbicides are not used in agriculture and where native diversity of soybeans exists. China, Taiwan, Japan, and Korea are regions where soybeans have evolved and where wild relatives of cultivated soybeans are found. In these regions, Monsanto's Roundup Ready soybeans would increase herbicide use and "pollute" the native biodiversity by transferring herbicide-resistant genes to wild plants. This could lead to new weed problems and loss of biodiversity. Moreover, since the Third World is the home to most of the world's biodiversity, the risks of genetic pollution in Third World countries are even more profound.

Herbicide-resistant transgenic crops can also become weeds when seeds from those crops germinate after harvest. More herbicides will have to be applied to eliminate these "volunteer plants."

Toxic Plants: A Recipe for Superpests

The bacterium *Bacillus thuringiensis* (Bt) was isolated from soil in 1911. Since 1930, it has been available as an organic form of pest control. Organic farmers have stepped up its use since the 1980s.

Monsanto and other "life sciences" corporations developed a technique of inserting the toxin-producing gene from the Bt bacteria into plants. This particular Bt gene produces a toxin that disables insects, and the genetically engineered Bt plants are thus able to produce their own pesticide. Genetically engineered Bt-crops have been cultivated commercially since 1996.

While Monsanto sells Bt-crops with the claim that they will reduce pesticide use, Bt-crops can actually create "superpests" and increase the need for pesticides. Bt-crops continuously express the Bt toxin throughout their growing season. Long-term exposure to the toxins promotes the development of resistance in insect populations. This kind of exposure could lead to selection for resistance in all stages of the insect pest on all parts of the plant for the entire season.

Due to these risks of encouraging pest resistance, the U.S. Environmental Protection Agency (EPA) offers only conditional and temporary registration for Bt-crops. The EPA requires a 4 percent refuge for Bt cotton—i.e., 4 percent of the cotton in a Bt-cotton field must be conventional and not express the Bt toxin. The conventional cotton acts as a refuge for insects to survive and breed in order to keep the overall level of resistance in the population low.

While the Monsanto propaganda states that farmers will not have to use pesticides, the reality is that the management of resistance requires continued use of non-Bt cotton and pesticide sprays. And even with a 4 percent refuge, insect resistance will evolve in as few as three to four years. Already eight species of insects have developed resistance to Bt toxins, including diamond black moth, Indian meal moth, tobacco budworm, colorado potato beetle, and two species of mosquitoes.

Even if Bt-crops do repel some pests, most crops have a diversity of insect pests. Insecticides will still have to be applied to control pests that are not susceptible to Bt's toxin. Beneficial species such as birds, bees, butterflies, and beetles, which are necessary for pollination and which through the prey-predator balance also control pests, may be threatened by Bt-crops. Soil-inhabiting organisms that degrade the toxin-contaminated organic matter can be harmed by the toxin. Nothing is known of the impact on human health when Bt-crops such as potato and corn are eaten, or on animal health when oilcake from Bt-cotton or fodder from Bt-corn is consumed as cattle feed. . . .

Genetic Engineering and Food Security

Diversity and high productivity go hand in hand if diverse outputs are taken into account and the costs of external inputs are added to the cost of inputs. The monoculture paradigm focuses on yields of single commodities and externalizes the costs of chemicals and energy. Inefficient and wasteful industrial agriculture are hence presented as efficient and productive.

The myth of increasing yields is the most common justification for introducing genetically engineered crops in agriculture. However, genetic engineering is actually leading to a "yield drag." On the basis of 8,200 university-based soybean trials in 1998, it was found that the top Roundup Ready soybean varieties had 4.6 bushels per acre, or yields 6.7 percent lower than the top conventional varieties. As environmental consultant Dr. Charles Benbrook states,

> In 1999, the Roundup Ready Soybean yield drag could result in perhaps a 2.0 to 2.5 percent reduction in national average soybean yields, compared to what they would have been if seed companies had not dramatically shifted breeding priorities to focus on herbicide tolerance. If not reversed by future breeding enhancements, this downward shift in soybean yield potential could emerge as the most significant decline in a major crop ever associated with a single genetic modification.

Research on trials with Bt cotton in India also showed a dramatic reduction in yields: in some cases as high as 75 percent.

As criticism of biotechnology's emphasis on herbicide-resistant crops and crops that produce toxins grows, the biotechnology industry has started to talk of engineering crops for nitrogen fixing, salinity tolerance, and high nutrition instead. However, all these traits already exist in farmers' varieties and farmers' fields. Legumes and pulses intercropped with cereals fix nitrogen. In coastal ecosystems, farmers have evolved a variety of salt-tolerant crops. We do not need genetic engineering to give us crops rich in nutrition. Amaranth has nine times more calcium than wheat and 40 times more calcium than rice. Its iron content is four times higher than that of rice, and it has twice as much protein. *Ragi* (finger millet) provides 35 times more calcium than rice, twice as much iron, and five times more minerals. Barnyard millet contains nine times more minerals than rice. Nutritious and resource-prudent crops such as millets and legumes are the best path of food security.

Biodiversity already holds the answers to many of the problems for which genetic engineering is being offered as a solution. Shifting from the monoculture mind to biodiversity, from the engineering paradigm to an ecological one, can help us conserve biodiversity, meet our needs for food and nutrition, and avoid the risks of genetic pollution.

"*Adherence to organic principles requires respect for [the] relationships [between species] that . . . sustain the biosphere—and thereby human existence.*"

Organic Farming Protects the Environment and Sustains Human Life

Jonathan Dimbleby

In the following viewpoint, Jonathan Dimbleby contends that organic farming protects the biodiversity that sustains human existence. According to Dimbleby, modern farming methods—which rely on toxic chemicals and single-crop cultivation—quickly exhaust the land and lead to the impoverishment of rural people. In contrast, he maintains, organic farming safeguards the environment and thereby protects the world's poorest people, who rely on the land for their livelihood. Jonathan Dimbleby is a British broadcaster and journalist.

As you read, consider the following questions:
1. According to Dimbleby, how do modern farmers specialize?
2. What specific factors cause environmental devastation, in the author's view?
3. As stated by the author, what can be found in one cubic meter of earth from an ancient beech forest?

A few years ago, few bothered about the organic movement except to mock the Prince of Wales for his pioneering contribution to what has now become a major debate about the crops we grow and the food we eat. Today, however, the organic movement is on a roller-coaster; the number of people who choose to grow or consume organic produce is rising at a dramatic rate, a phenomenon that is forcing everyone involved at every stage in the food chain to rethink the basic assumptions of the last 50 years.

Yet despite this growth, this rapid reassessment of recent agricultural developments, the organic movement has its critics and they are loud and insistent. 'Organic farming cannot feed an ever-increasing global population,' they shout; 'It cannot weather the inconsistencies of climate', they continue; and they conclude with the ever-common mantra: 'It's just too expensive'.

The critics of the organic movement have much to say, and before I continue, I must be honest. There was once a time when I may have been among their number.

From Childhood Acres to Factory Farms

I was brought up on a small farm in Sussex. I took it all for granted. The cats, the dogs, the ponies, the cows, the pigs, the chickens and two geese ominously named Christmas Day and Boxing Day who grew very old and fierce—because, when the moment arrived, no-one had had the temerity to take the action required to turn them into a feast. On our farm, chemical fertilisers were still a novelty, referred to disparagingly as 'artificial'. Pesticides, similarly, were unknown: docks, nettles and thistles were scythed away by hand just as they came into seed. Antibiotics were a last resort, not an addiction. We did not use the term organic; indeed I had never heard of it.

I decided I wanted to be a farmer. I went to agricultural college and remember trying to create on paper a profitable farm business. I soon discovered that it was—apparently—impossible both to make money and to recreate the traditional character of my childhood acres. The figures simply didn't stack up. To succeed, I discovered, you had to specialise.

You needed vast acres of corn or an intensive dairy farm

with scores if not hundreds of cows—thin and spindly creatures, invariably black and white in colour with pendulous udders, designed and constructed by geneticists to produce vast quantities of milk in the most efficient way possible.

Or you could have battery chickens in the hundreds of thousands, caged and cramped to prevent them moving around freely and thus expending wasteful energy that should be more profitably deployed either laying an egg a day or getting fat as fast as possible. Or pigs, sows tethered in stalls, piglets weaned early and reared in the semi-dark on wooden slats in a humid atmosphere that reeked of dung and urine. It was a world in which farmers were required to be permanently at war—zapping the enemy that lurked in the soil, in the hedges, trees and ponds, in the very air itself, with an awesome selection of chemical firepower. Victory would be secured with pesticides, herbicides, and fungicides. And, in the case of livestock, with the wonder of antibiotics used on a daily basis both to promote growth and to prevent disease.

Brave New World

It was a brave new world and it was remarkably seductive. Food would be plentiful and cheap and we would all live happily ever after. I bought the argument hook, line and sinker. I even wrote an article which wire published in the college magazine suggesting that the vista was not only attractive but exceedingly profitable. And I castigated the farming community for moaning all the way to the bank with their huge subsidy cheques from the British taxpayer.

Anyway, I soon found myself on another primrose path. Via university and into television where I spent a great deal of time travelling the world from one crisis or disaster to another. In India, Latin America, but especially in Africa, and there, particularly in Ethiopia, I saw the horrific consequences of what were then widely regarded as natural disasters. The rains failing; the droughts; the seed perishing on the stalk; no grain. People starving.

In Ethiopia in 1973, I stumbled across human suffering on a scale that I could scarcely believe. People dead and dying on the roadside and in makeshift camps in the towns and villages round about. I saw piles of bodies waiting to be buried; entire families; mothers and fathers, children and tiny babies. To witness such things—a young mother grieving for the dead baby she still clasped to her chest—reminded me of the concentration camp at Belsen [Germany, during World War II], the full horror of which was revealed to the world in 1945 by my father. No-one thought that Belsen was a natural disaster: everyone knew that it was the calculated consequence of an evil vision.

Share of Farmland Under Organic Management, 2000

Country/Region	Percent
Australia	10.4
Switzerland	8.3
Finland	7.1
Italy	6.2
Denmark	6.0
Sweden	5.5
EU average	2.8
Germany	2.6
Canada	1.3
United States	0.2
Argentina	0.2

Compiled from various sources by Worldwatch.

It seemed to me that this first famine in Ethiopia, or rather the first to attract a huge international response—whilst very different from the crime against humanity perpetrated at Belsen—was not possible to explain away, glibly and forgivingly, as a natural disaster.

It is true that the rains had failed. But the soil was also eroding fast. Trees and forests had been cut down to provide fuel and even the most fertile soils were eroding at an alarming rate. Water storage and irrigation systems were notable by their absence. And it was also noticeable that only the poor succumbed while the rich—the landowners, the merchants, the officials, the ministers and the generals—continued to prosper.

So I met people who know better, and I read, and I learnt a little. And as a result I came to the view that almost no disaster was natural—and that the environmental devastation was both cause and effect: the product of a complex set of interwoven causes—among the most obvious of which were poverty, injustice, corruption, repression and war. A vicious circle and a vortex for hundreds of millions of innocent people.

To put it another way: we must treat the planet as if we are going to live for ever and not as though we had simply dropped in for a weekend break. I think that is a pretty good rule of thumb, litmus test and guide to action. The phrase used today to describe this approach is 'sustainable development'.

What I've seen in the poorest parts of the poorest countries of the Third World over the last 25 years offers a crucial challenge to the notion of sustainable development. You cannot have sustainable development anywhere on earth when the great majority of the global population is getting poorer while the rest of us get richer. That is a recipe for disaster, not development. If it is to mean anything at all, sustainable development must be about fairness in the use of the resources on which we all depend for survival.

And that, for me, is where sustainable development meets the organic movement. Essential to the idea of organic production is the belief that it is possible to work with nature, not against nature. That you can produce high quality and nutritious food without zapping every predator in sight. That good timing and sensible crop rotation, combined with a respect for bio-diversity, is the most sustainable form of agriculture possible: protecting the environment, enhancing human health, and—incidentally—strengthening, not weakening, the social and economic fabric of rural communities.

The Chain of Life

Organic production is based on the principle that, in the chain of life on earth, no species is irrelevant and all are interdependent: from bacteria to fungi, from insects to vertebrates. Adherence to organic principles requires respect for these intricate relationships that between them sustain the biosphere—and thereby human existence.

A measure of that intricacy is the fact that if you scoop up one cubic metre of earth from an ancient beech forest, you will find no fewer than 50,000 small earthworms, 50,000 insects and mites, and 12 million roundworms. From one gramme of that soil you might unearth some 30,000 protozoa, 50,000 algae, 400,000 fungi and billions of individual bacteria of unknown species.

The American poet, farmer and philosopher, Wendell Berry, writes of this organic life in the soil in lyrical, almost spiritual, terms:

'The soil is the healer and restorer and resurrector by which disease passes into health, age into youth, death into life. Without proper care for it we can have no community, because without proper care for it we can have no life.

'It is alive itself. It is a grave, too, of course. Or a healthy soil is. It is full of dead animals and plants, bodies that have passed through other bodies. . . the only way into the soil is through other bodies. But no matter how freely the dead are broken down, or how many times they are eaten, they yet give into other life. If a healthy soil is full of death it is also full of life. . . Given only the health of the soil nothing that dies is dead for very long.'

Protecting Biodiversity

The Prince of Wales is fond of saying that seeing is believing. And when you see organic crops in the field, you know what he means. I have seen a field of beans, black and sticky with aphids. You think that the crop must be doomed. And then three months later the aphids have entirely disappeared. And the crop looks wonderful.

What has happened? No, not a drop of pesticide. No dust from any fungicide. The work has been done by ladybirds [ladybugs]. Ladybirds which have come into life in the surrounding hedgerows, protected in a chemical-free environment and, as nature dictates, moved in en masse to wipe out the aphids and clean up the crop. It happens year after year. Natural predation; no chemicals.

In this context, I am a touch perplexed by Sir John Krebs, the new head of the [British] Food Standards Agency, who seems to me to have been rather less well-advised than might have been good for him. How can he be so certain as to instruct the public—as he did on a recent British Broadcasting Company (BBC) Country File programme—that consumers are wasting their money if they think they are getting extra safety by buying organic? Why is he so dismissive? I am sure that he has not been nobbled. Yet he has allowed himself to rush into judgement.

A growing body of research demonstrates that the beneficial effects of organic farming in protecting biodiversity go much wider. Indeed, there is evidence to show what organic producers have long suspected: that organic farming methods are an exceptionally effective way of protecting the wildlife of rural Britain.

For my own part, I end almost where I started—with thoughts of local farming, and my own process of learning. I once thought that intensive farming was the way ahead— the more you grow, the more you feed; everyone's happy. But in those young years of mine I was viewing agriculture in an isolated context, failing to see that farms are not just providers of food, but intrinsic human relationships with the world around us all. The more I read and saw, the more the bigger picture began to reveal itself.

For me, organic agriculture is destined to play a crucial part in that big picture: helping to create a future in which those who follow us—our children and our children's children—will be able to look back and say, 'they did us proud'.

"The first consequence of a global shift to organic farming would be the plowdown of at least six-million square miles of wildlife habitat to make up for . . . lower yields."

Organic Farming Harms the Environment and Threatens Human Health

Dennis T. Avery

Dennis T. Avery argues in the following viewpoint that foods produced by organic farming have caused countless deaths due to their high concentration of deadly bacterium such as E. coli and salmonella. Moreover, Avery contends that an increase in organic farming would harm the environment by decreasing biodiversity. Since organic farming produces lower food yields than modern farming, Avery maintains, more wildlife habitat would have to be converted to farmland to feed a growing world population. Dennis T. Avery is director of Global Food Issues for the Hudson Institute, a public policy research center, and the author of *Saving the Planet With Pesticides and Plastic: The Environmental Triumph of High-Yield Farming.*

As you read, consider the following questions:

1. According to Avery, how many times more likely are people who eat organic food to be attacked by E. coli 0157:H7 than those who do not consume such foods?
2. How do the yields of organic farming compare to the yields of modern farming, as reported by the author?
3. How does Avery support his assertion that modern pesticides do not pose a significant risk to wildlife?

P roducts most people think are purer than other foods are making people seriously ill.

Deadly Organic Foods

According to recent data compiled by the U.S. Centers for Disease Control (CDC), people who eat organic and "natural" foods are eight times as likely as the rest of the population to be attacked by a deadly new strain of E. coli bacteria (0157: H7). This new E. coli is attacking tens of thousands of people per year, all over the world. It is causing permanent liver and kidney damage in many of its victims. The CDC recorded 2,471 confirmed cases of E. coli 0157:H7 in 1996 and estimated that it is causing at least 250 deaths per year in the United States alone.

Consumers of organic food are also more likely to be attacked by a relatively new, more virulent strain of the infamous salmonella bacteria. Salmonella was America's biggest food-borne death risk until the new E. coli 0157 came along.

Killer Manure

Organic food is more dangerous than conventionally grown produce because organic farmers use animal manure as the major source of fertilizer for their food crops. Animal manure is the biggest reservoir of these nasty bacteria that are afflicting and killing so many people.

Organic farmers compound the contamination problem through their reluctance to use antimicrobial preservatives, chemical washes, pasteurization, or even chlorinated water to rid their products of dangerous bacteria. One organic grower summed up the community's attitude as follows: "Pasteurization has only been around a hundred years or so; what do they think people did before that?"

The answer is simple. They died young.

In truth, until the last few years the threat of food-borne bacteria was relatively mild in the U.S. It was prudent to refrigerate one's food and wash one's hands before preparing food or eating, and those simple procedures kept food-borne illnesses to a minimum. On occasion, neglect of these rules would cause a family to suffer severe stomach aches. And every year a few weak individuals—the very young, the very old, or those who were already quite ill—would die from exposure to food-borne bacteria.

But the new E. coli attacks even the strong. It inflicts permanent damage on internal organs. It even kills healthy adults. The new salmonella is nearly as dangerous.

Harsh Organic Reality

As these lethal new bacteria spread, organic foods have clearly become the deadliest food choice. Put simply, animal manure is too dangerous to use on food crops if there is any alternative whatever. To eat produce grown with animal fertilizer is like playing Russian roulette with your family's dinner table. It only takes one contaminated food product to bring on a tragedy.

"I was really horrified that something I felt was so wholesome and so healthy and so safe for my children could really almost kill them," said Rita Bernstein, a Connecticut housewife. In 1996, two of Bernstein's three daughters suffered E. coli 0157 attacks that were traced to organic lettuce. Halee, the younger daughter, is still suffering from reduced kidney function and vision problems. Bernstein is grateful that her daughters are still alive. "There are a lot of families out there that don't have their Halees," she says.

The new reality is quite sobering. Organic and "natural" food producers supply only about 1 percent of the nation's food, but the Centers for Disease Control have traced approximately 8 percent of the confirmed E. coli 0157 cases to such foods. Consumer Reports recently found much higher levels of salmonella on free-range chickens than on conventionally raised ones. Many other organic foods also pose higher salmonella risks than "supermarket" foods. To be sure, most strains of salmonella are mild and are easily killed by cooking one's food adequately. But the new salmonella, S. typhimurium, is far stronger than other varieties. Infection often proves fatal. The CDC estimates that there are up to four million cases of salmonella poisoning per year in the U.S., and it has identified one-fourth of the culture-confirmed cases as the more virulent S. typhimurium.

As if that were not frightening enough, organic and "natural" food consumers also face increased risk of illness from toxins produced by fungi—and some of these toxins are carcinogenic. Refusing to use artificial pesticides, organic farmers allow their crop fields to suffer more damage from insects and rodents, which creates openings through which fungi can enter the fruits and seeds. The U.S. Food and Drug Administration (FDA) regularly tests samples of various foods for such dangers, and it routinely finds high levels of these natural toxins in organically grown produce. It found, for instance, that organic crops have higher rates of infestation by aflatoxin, one of the most virulent carcinogens known to man. Unfortunately, the FDA has issued no public warnings about these risks so far.

The organic-food sector stresses the "natural" production of foods and beverages—even to the point of refusing to pasteurize milk and fruit juices. As a result, many people become seriously ill after consuming products they mistakenly believe are purer than other foods. For instance, in 1996 E. coli 0157 sickened more than seventy people who contracted it from unpasteurized apple juice produced by the Odwalla Juice Company. One young girl in Colorado died because of this. Odwalla was recently fined more than $1 million in the case and now pasteurizes its juice. But more than 1,500 other companies still cater to the "natural means raw" idea by selling unpasteurized beverages that can prove deadly.

Even without pesticides and pasteurization, producers could render their organic and natural foods safe through a well-known process called irradiation. Irradiation uses low levels of gamma radiation to kill bacteria, and the process also preserves the freshness of foods such as strawberries and chicken. But when the U.S. Department of Agriculture (USDA) recently proposed an organic-food standard that would have allowed irradiation, the plan drew more than 200,000 angry protests from organic farmers and caterers. In response, the USDA will eliminate irradiation from the final organic food standard.

Fresh from the Manure Pile

To be sure, it is an overstatement to say, as one physician recently did, that organic food is "grown in animal manure." Few organic farmers actually put fresh manure on their crops. Most of them compost the manure for several weeks before using it on their crops. But the composting guidelines have been fuzzy and are probably inadequate. A common rule of thumb is to compost for two months at 130 degrees F. or better. The bad news is that a study by Dr. Dean Cliver of the University of California at Davis found that the deadly new E. coli 0157 bacteria can live at least seventy days in a compost pile—and it probably takes an extended period at 160-degree heat to kill it.

Organic Farming Can Harm Workers

The assumption of many who buy organics is that growers treat their workers with as much care as they do their tender shoots and berries. In fact, . . . [a]lthough organic growers, pickers, and packagers are spared the exposure to toxic pesticides they would endure on regular farms, labor inspection reports show that they often toil in dangerous, unsanitary conditions for wages that sometimes don't approach the legal minimum. "Just because you're buying organic doesn't mean the labor practices are any better at all," says former legal aid attorney Gary Restaino.

Kit R. Roane, *U.S. News & World Report*, April 22, 2002.

Few organic farmers use thermometers to check the safety of their compost piles, or even keep accurate records on how long a given mass of compost has been sitting. For most organic farmers, management of their natural fertilizer is a casual matter of shifting compost piles around with a tractor-mounted front-end loader.

The real surprise is that nobody is telling the public about the new dangers from organic food, or trying to persuade organic farmers to reduce these risks. Activist groups, government, and the press—all of which have shown no reluctance to organize crusades about matters such as global warming, tobacco addiction, and the use of pesticides—are allowing organic farmers to endanger their customers without any publicity whatever. A press corps eager to find headline-worthy dangers would long ago have exposed any other farmers guilty of so blatantly and unnecessarily endangering the public. And other farmers would certainly have been condemned, or even closed down, by government regulators.

Politically Favored

Organic foods, however, are politically favored. The Green lobby self-righteously protects them because it urgently wants the public to perceive organic farming as an environmentally benign alternative to the use of pesticides and chemical fertilizers. I recently criticized organic farming on a Canadian Broadcasting Corporation program, and the network was peppered with protest calls before the program even went on the air!

Even newspaper food editors still tell their readers that organic food is chic, healthy, and "earth-friendly." In general, the U.S. press has been blithely abetting the scare tactics of the environmental movement for decades, and the food writers pride themselves on being at least as "green" as their colleagues on the news pages.

With truly mind-numbing aggressiveness, the organic farming advocates have even gone so far as to claim that "industrial farming" created E. coli 0157. They argue that consumers should protect themselves by buying organic products from local farmers, a "recommendation" that blatantly serves their own self-interest. The truth is, no one knows where the new E. coli strain came from, but we do know that bacteria are constantly mutating as a natural consequence of their rapid reproduction. Allowing bacteria to proliferate, as organic farmers do, is not the way to minimize mutations.

Strangely Silent Regulators

Federal regulators have largely been cowed into silence. The intensity with which organic-farming believers and eco-activists defend their old-fashioned type of agriculture rivals the intensity of the religious fanatic. For instance, one consumer recently said, "I think trying to eliminate the poisons and pesticides from our food is a great way to eliminate the chemical industry's destruction of the earth." As a consequence of such attitudes, the CDC has neglected its responsibility to warn the public about the newly increased dangers of organic foods. One CDC doctor—Dr. Robert Tauxe, Chief of the CDC's Food-Borne Diseases Branch—wrote an article in the *Journal of the American Medical Association* (May 8, 1997) highlighting the dangers of "organically grown, unprocessed foods produced without pesticides or preservatives." The CDC was promptly flooded with angry phone calls from passionate believers in organic farming. The doctor now says that he "doesn't know" whether organic food is more dangerous than conventionally produced food. The CDC has refused to grant interviews on the subject.

With similar obtuseness, the U.S. Environmental Protection Agency (EPA) has recently issued a draft of a new consumer brochure highlighting the unproven "dangers" from pesticide residues—and recommending organic foods. But after forty years and billions of dollars in research, scientists are still looking for the first victim of pesticide residues, whereas the new E. coli strain attacked thousands of Americans last year. Many of these victims suffered permanent internal organ damage, and hundreds of them died. The EPA's draft brochure on pesticide residues simply appears to reflect the antipesticide biases of the agency's [former] administrator, Carol Browner, and her political patron, [former] Vice President Al Gore.

Other federal agencies have displayed the same bias. The Food and Drug Administration, for instance, has failed to issue any warnings to consumers about the higher levels of natural toxins their researchers regularly find in organic foods. And the Department of Agriculture, which employs some of the world's best food scientists, goes out of its way to court the organic-farming supporters and allied eco-activists, and makes a strenuous effort to find good things to say about "alternative agriculture."

Not "Earth-Friendly"

"Natural food" proponents claim that organic farming is "earth-friendly," but it's not. The ugly secret of organic farming is that its yields are only about half as high as those of mainstream farmers. Approximately one-third of the average organic farm is not planted to marketable crops at all; it is planted to green manure crops (such as clover) to build up the nitrogen fertility of the soil. If the organic farmers gave up animal manure as a nitrogen source, the percentage of land they keep in green manure crops would have to become even higher. Mainstream farmers take their nitrogen from the air, through an industrial process that requires no land to be taken from nature.

Also, the organic farmers suffer higher losses from destruction by pests. They expect it. Books on organic farming tell their readers to live with it. "I'm lucky to get half as much yield from my organic acres as from my regular fields," said the manager of a 50,000-acre cooperative farm in England. His experience is confirmed by numerous studies from a dozen different countries.

Need for Higher Yields

For all these reasons, widespread organic farming is simply not a viable option at this time. The first consequence of a global shift to organic farming would be the plowdown of at least six-million square miles of wildlife habitat to make up for the lower yields of organic production. That is more than the total land area of the United States.

Agriculture already takes up 36 percent of the world's land surface. (All the world's cities cover only 1.5 percent.) A world with a peak population of 8.5 billion affluent people in 2050 will need at least 2.5 times as much farm output as we have today.

Absent a worldwide catastrophe involving billions of human deaths, this demand is inevitable. We will not be able to count on people to change their diets and accept less protein. There is no global trend toward vegetarianism today, nor any sign of one. In America, for example, less than 4 percent of the population is vegetarian, and 95 percent of U.S. vegetarians consume milk, cheese, eggs, and other expensive calories. Less than 0.05 percent of the affluent people in the world give up livestock products completely.

In fact, the worldwide trend is in the opposite direction. Countries such as China, India, and South Korea are leading the biggest surge in demand for meat and milk the world has ever seen. It is now probably too late to save wildlands by preventing people from acquiring a taste for meat and milk, and there is certainly no sign of mass conversions to vegetarianism around the globe.

If the world does not triple the yields on the high-quality land currently in farming, we will pay the price not in human famine but in forests and wild meadows cleared to produce more meat, milk, and produce.

The Benefits of Pesticides

Modern farm chemicals are not entirely without risk, but the hazards they pose to people and wildlife are near zero and declining. For instance, Captan, one of the pesticides on the Greenpeace hit list, is one ten-millionth as carcinogenic as ordinary drinking water. EPA Administrator Browner is trying to decertify an herbicide called atrazine because a few parts per billion turn up in some of our drinking water. But Browner's own staff concedes that to get above the "no-effect" level in the rat tests that ascertain cancer risk, you would have to drink 150,000 gallons of water per day for seventy years. And for nine months of the year you would have to add your own atrazine! The health risks of modern pesticides are minimal.

Nonetheless, advocates of organic farming like to ask, "What's more dangerous, pesticides or horse manure?" The answer may surprise them. Researchers are still looking for the first human death from pesticide residues, fifty years after DDT was introduced and thirty years after its use was banned in the United States, but manure is apparently claiming lives almost daily through bacterial contamination of organic food.

Nor do modern pesticides pose a significant risk to wildlife. They are more narrowly targeted, degrade more rapidly, and are better designed to avoid wildlife impact than the early, more persistent pesticides. Also, they are often used in integrated pest management systems to minimize the amount and frequency of treatments, and are applied with computer-calculated precision. The new glyphosate and sulfanylurea weed killers are no more toxic to birds and fish than table salt, and one tiny tablet treats an entire acre. Quite simply, when used properly these substances are not dangerous to anything but the pests they are designed to regulate.

Giving up pesticides would mean the certain destruction of millions of square miles of wildlands, much of it in the species-rich tropics. Because much of the world's biodiversity is in those lands, a move toward widespread organic farming would cost nature far more than the careful use of today's safe, narrowly targeted pesticides, high-powered seeds, and factory-produced fertilizers.

Organic food buyers are, unfortunately, twice losers: They and their families accept deadly risks from truly dangerous new food-borne microorganisms, and, at the same time, their choices increase the likelihood that the people of the next century will plow down massive tracts of wildlife habitat to make way for low-yield crops.

Unless the press and government agencies fulfill their obligation to warn people of the dangers of these foods, the number of such incidents will continue to rise. These risks are easy to overcome, but farmers and consumers must know the dangers and act accordingly.

*"The era of mass-produced animal flesh,
and its unsustainable costs to human and
environmental health, should be over
before the next century is out."*

Livestock Agriculture Depletes Land Resources

Ed Ayres

Ed Ayres maintains in the following viewpoint that the waste produced by cattle, pigs, and chickens is polluting the world's supply of fresh water. Moreover, growing grain to feed cattle uses significantly more of the Earth's decreasing freshwater supply than growing grain to feed people. According to Ayres, livestock agriculture also threatens human health due to the high bacteria and cholesterol content of factory-farmed meat. Ayres contends that mass-producing animal flesh leads to deforestation and the loss of wildlife habitat. Ed Ayres is editorial director of the Worldwatch Institute, a research organization that analyzes global problems, and author of *God's Last Offer: Negotiating for a Sustainable Future*.

As you read, consider the following questions:

1. What percentage of the wheat, corn, and other grain produced in the United States goes to feeding herds of livestock, as stated by Ayres?
2. As reported by the author, what diseases are associated with meat-heavy diets?
3. According to Ayres, what features of human physiology will enable people to adapt to a meat-free diet?

When Julius Caesar made his triumphal entrance into Rome in 45 B.C., he celebrated by giving a feast at which thousands of guests gorged on poultry, seafood and game. Similar celebrations featuring exorbitant consumption of animal flesh have marked human victories—in war, sport, politics and commerce—since our species learned to control fire. Throughout the developing world today, one of the first things people do as they climb out of poverty is to shift from their peasant diet of mainly grains and beans to one that is rich in pork or beef. Since 1950, per capita consumption of meat around the globe has more than doubled.

Meat, it seems, is not just food but reward as well. But in the coming century, that will change. Much as we have awakened to the full economic and social costs of cigarettes, we will find we can no longer subsidize or ignore the costs of mass-producing cattle, poultry, pigs, sheep and fish to feed our growing population. These costs include hugely inefficient use of freshwater and land, heavy pollution from livestock feces, rising rates of heart disease and other degenerative illnesses, and spreading destruction of the forests on which much of our planet's life depends.

First, consider the impact on supplies of freshwater. To produce 1 lb. of feedlot beef requires 7 lbs. of feed grain, which takes 7,000 lbs. of water to grow. Pass up one hamburger, and you'll save as much water as you save by taking 40 showers with a low-flow nozzle. Yet in the U.S., 70% of all the wheat, corn and other grain produced goes to feeding herds of livestock. Around the world, as more water is diverted to raising pigs and chickens instead of producing crops for direct consumption, millions of wells are going dry. India, China, North Africa and the U.S. are all running freshwater deficits, pumping more from their aquifers than rain can replenish. As populations in water-scarce regions continue to expand, governments will inevitably act to cut these deficits by shifting water to grow food, not feed. The new policies will raise the price of meat to levels unaffordable for any but the rich.

That prospect will doubtless provoke protests that direct consumption of grain can't provide the same protein that meat provides. Indeed, it can't. But nutritionists will attest that most people in the richest countries don't need nearly as much protein as we're currently getting from meat, and there are plenty of vegetable sources—including the grains now squandered on feed—that can provide the protein we need.

An Environmental Issue

A global switch to meat-based diets and factory farming methods is very much an environmental issue, both because of widespread land degradation as a result of overgrazing and the increasing diversion of world grain supplies and productive farm land to feed a burgeoning population of domesticated animals. China, for instance, fed 17 percent of its grain to livestock in 1985; by 1994, that figure had risen to 23 percent. In the U.S.—the model—70 percent of the grain produced is fed to animals. As Dr. Robert Lawrence of the new Johns Hopkins Center for a Livable Future points out, "The inefficiency of converting eight or nine kilograms of grain protein into one kilogram of animal protein for human consumption would by itself be sufficient argument against continuation of our present dietary habits."

Jim Motavalli and Tracey C. Rembert, *E Magazine*, May 15, 1998.

Unfortunately, this isn't just a matter of productive capacity. Mass production of meat has also become a staggering source of pollution. Maybe cow pies were once just a pastoral joke, but in recent years livestock waste has been implicated in massive fish kills and outbreaks of such diseases as pfiesteria, which causes memory loss, confusion and acute skin burning in people exposed to contaminated water. In the U.S., livestock now produce 130 times as much waste as people do. Just one hog farm in Utah, for example, produces more sewage than the city of Los Angeles. These megafarms are proliferating, and in populous areas their waste is tainting drinking water. In more pristine regions, from Indonesia to the Amazon, tropical rain forest is being burned down to make room for more and more cattle. Agriculture is the world's biggest cause of deforestation, and increasing demand for meat is the biggest force in the expansion of agriculture.

What has proved an unsustainable burden to the life of the planet is also proving unsustainable for the planet's dominant species. In China a recent shift to meat-heavy diets has been linked to increases in obesity, cardiovascular disease, breast cancer and colorectal cancer. U.S. and World Health Organization researchers have announced similar findings for other parts of the world. And then there are the growing concerns about what happens to people who eat the flesh of animals that have been pumped full of genetically modified organisms, hormones and antibiotics.

These concerns may seem counterintuitive. We evolved as hunter-gatherers and ate meat for a hundred millenniums before modern times. It's natural for us to eat meat, one might say. But today's factory-raised, transgenic, chemical-laden livestock are a far cry from the wild animals our ancestors hunted. When we cleverly shifted from wildland hunting and gathering to systematic herding and farming, we changed the natural balances irrevocably. The shift enabled us to produce food surpluses, but the surpluses also allowed us to reproduce prodigiously. When we did, it became only a matter of time before we could no longer have the large area of wildland, per individual, that is necessary to sustain a top-predator species.

By covering more and more of the planet with our cities, farms and waste, we have jeopardized other top predators that need space as well. Tigers and panthers are being squeezed out and may not last the coming century. We, at least, have the flexibility—the omnivorous stomach and creative brain—to adapt. We can do it by moving down the food chain: eating foods that use less water and land, and that pollute far less, than cows and pigs do. In the long run, we can lose our memory of eating animals, and we will discover the intrinsic satisfactions of a diverse plant-based diet, as millions of people already have.

I'm not predicting the end of all meat eating. Decades from now, cattle will still be raised, perhaps in patches of natural rangeland, for people inclined to eat and able to afford a porterhouse, while others will make exceptions in ceremonial meals on special days like Thanksgiving, which link us ritually to our evolutionary and cultural past. But the era of mass-produced animal flesh, and its unsustainable costs to human and environmental health, should be over before the next century is out.

"Cattle help feed a hungry world by converting water and nutrients into a highly nutrient-dense food."

Livestock Agriculture Is Beneficial

National Cattlemen's Beef Association

The National Cattlemen's Beef Association (NCBA) is the marketing organization and trade association for America's 1 million cattle farmers and ranchers. In the following viewpoint, the association claims that producing meat helps feed the world's people and protect the environment. The NCBA asserts that cows are able to convert nutrients not suitable for human consumption into highly nutritious food. In consequence, according to the association, lands that are unsuitable for growing crops can be utilized for grazing cattle, which increases the world's percentage of food-producing acres. Contrary to what many critics claim, the association contends, livestock agriculture does not pollute rivers, erode soil, or harm wildlife.

As you read, consider the following questions:
1. What percentage of the world's beef supply is produced by the United States, according to the NCBA?
2. As stated by the association, how do ruminants increase the world's food supply?
3. How do cattlemen contribute to wildlife production, in the association's opinion?

Cattle help feed a hungry world by converting water and nutrients into a highly nutrient-dense food. These nutrients used by cattle are, for the most part, unsuitable for human consumption.

U.S. cattlemen and other agricultural producers are committed to caring for America's environmental resources, which are essential to feeding the nation and the world. In fact, less than 2 percent of the U.S. population feeds this country and 70 million other people around the globe. Central to this success story is the dedication of U.S. cattlemen and the inherent ability of cattle to efficiently convert certain natural resources, often unfit for any other purpose, into protein for humans. Cattlemen in the United States produce about one-fourth of the world's beef supply with only about 10% of the world's cattle population. This efficiency is achieved by wise use of the natural resources, soil and water, upon which the cattle industry is dependent upon for its very survival. The nutrients fed to cattle are often unsuitable for human consumption, thereby providing a valuable service by converting these nutrients to a food of high nutritional value for human consumption. The primary renewable resources are solar energy, water and forage. Those are not used up, but are naturally replenished on a continual basis.

Grazing

Cattle grazing is an efficient way to produce food for human use on land where crops for human consumption cannot be produced. The use of land to graze animals more than doubles the land area in this country that can be used to produce food. . . .

Food can only be harvested from the majority of America's more than 800 million acres of grazing land via ruminant (four-stomach) animals, such as cattle. Better than 90 percent of these rangelands are too high, too rough, too wet or too dry to grow cultivated crops. American rangelands are in better condition today than at the turn of the century because of farmers' and ranchers' commitment to sound stewardship. . . .

Grazing is an efficient use of a renewable resource. In fact, all rangeland evolved because of ruminant grazing. Cattle play a central role in the miraculous chain of sun to grass to human food. Grazing utilizes one of this country's most abundant, natural, renewable resources. Ruminants have the ability to efficiently convert low-energy grasses and other forage into nutritious, high-protein beef. Compared with harvested or purchased feeds, ranges and pastures provide a relatively inexpensive and energy-efficient feed source for livestock production. . . .

Cattle consume less than two-tenths of 1 percent of all water used in the United States. In fact, grassland areas best used by cattle actually contribute to increased water quality.

Considering all factors in beef cattle production, including direct consumption, irrigation of pastures and crops and carcass processing, it takes approximately 440 gallons of water to produce a pound of boneless beef in the United States. Irrigated pasture and crops fed to beef cattle account for only about 5 percent of all water used in the United States.

Grassland soils are an excellent biological filter to recover nutrients passing through the soil. Grass roots are active almost year-around and can recover nutrients from the soil that are leached out from other land uses. Water quality improves as grassland vegetation becomes denser and soil conditions improve. A University of Wisconsin study showed that grasslands are the best crop for reducing run-off, erosion and phosphorous pollution. . . .

It is illegal to discharge livestock waste into rivers, streams and lakes. Eighty-six percent of fed cattle marketed are produced in feedlots required to obtain National Pollution Discharge Elimination System (NPDES) permits by the federal Clean Water Act. Essentially, all beef cattle manure in feedlots is collected, loaded, hauled and applied as a natural organic fertilizer to soil directly or via storage/treatment systems. Management of feedlot surfaces, use of storage lagoons and holding ponds and other management practices have helped prevent runoff and groundwater contamination problems. Tests show that groundwater quality in cattle feeding regions remains high. . . .

Air Quality

Air quality is, at the most, minimally affected by beef production. While cattle are often the scapegoats for air quality issues, their manner of converting grass into protein may actually contribute to improved air quality. Grazing land plants remove carbon dioxide from the air through the process of photosynthesis and store it in the soil. Grazing land soils in the Great Plains have been found to contain over 40 tons of carbon per acre while cultivated soils contain 26 tons per acre. In addition, carbon dioxide emissions from a conventionally tilled field can be nine times higher than from no-till areas.

Manufacturing and Processing Uses of Water

Processing a quarter pound of hamburger . . . . .1 gallon
Processing a can of vegetables . . . . .9.3 gallons
Processing a chicken . . . . .11.6 gallons
Processing a barrel of beer . . . . .1,500 gallons
Refining a barrel of crude oil . . . . .1,851 gallons
Processing a ton of cane sugar . . . . .28,100 gallons
Manufacturing a car .39,090 gallons
Producing a ton of steel . . . . .62,600 gallons

National Cattlemen's Beef Association, 2002.

Some have questioned the role cattle production plays, specifically methane gas from cattle, in the deterioration of the ozone layer. Of the U.S. greenhouse gas emissions in 1997, 2.2 percent was methane produced by cattle. Other sources, such as landfills, the no. 1 source, accounted for 71.55% of U.S. methane emissions in 1997. Environmental scientists have overstated the immediacy of most environmental problems. For example, they would have us believe we must stay indoors or risk skin cancer due to a growing hole in the ozone layer. They fail to mention that the hole over the Arctic Circle was twice as severe in 1958 as it is today.

The major sources of methane gas include rice paddies, wetlands, biomass burning, fossil fuel exploration, landfills and coal mines, not cattle belching. . . .

Soil Conservation

Cattle production is not a major factor in soil erosion. In fact, increased production of forage and the use of grazing animals, such as cattle, to produce food offer a viable way to conserve soil while also producing food for human consumption. American cattlemen are committed to soil conservation and the prevention of soil erosion. Soil productivity, as well as water and air quality, is better maintained under the permanent vegetative cover of well-managed grazing lands than virtually any other land-use system.

Grass cover, such as that found on pastures and rangelands, prevents erosion. Natural causes, such as geological formations, hydrology, snow melt, flooding, droughts and other factors contribute significantly to erosion in this country.

Only 24 percent of the erosion from private rural lands is from pastures (3 percent) and rangelands (21 percent). Or, less than 14 percent of all erosion, from all types of land, is from pastures and range. The production of grains and harvested forages for all beef cattle accounts for only 5.8 percent of soil erosion from privately owned land.

Wildlife

Cattle production contributes to wildlife production. Management practices by cattlemen provide habitat for many species of wildlife. In addition, most cattlemen implement practices that specifically benefit wildlife that share their land. Seventy-five percent of wildlife habitat in the 48 contiguous states is on private lands. In 1995, 87 percent of cattlemen reported areas on their farms or ranches that support wildlife, compared with only 80 percent in 1990. Sixty-two percent of cattlemen also reported more wildlife on their land in 1995 than 10 years previous.

The improving trend in range condition has allowed striking increases in wildlife numbers. In the last 30 years elk have increased almost 800 percent, Bighorn sheep have increased 435 percent, antelope 112 percent, moose almost 500 percent, and deer by about one-third.

Because of their permanent and diverse plant cover, grasslands provide good habitat for wildlife. Research consistently shows that ground-nesting birds and small mammals thrive in properly managed pastures. Research also shows that grazing animals, such as deer and cattle, can be used to manage stream bank vegetation to enhance fish populations. Such studies in Minnesota and Wisconsin found fish populations two to three times greater in streams located in pastures where cattle grazed compared to streams located in pastures where cattle were totally excluded. . . .

Energy Efficiency

Compared to many other foods, beef is energy-efficient. More than 80 percent of the energy involved in food production, processing and preparation is used after food leaves the farm. Because many plant-source foods require large amounts of energy in the processing phase, the overall energy efficiency of beef often is comparable, or even superior, to the energy efficiency of plant-source foods. The energy required to produce soybeans is less than that to produce beef, but the processing required to produce soy protein isolate, the basis of meat substitutes, is an energy-intensive process. It is estimated that the energy used to produce 1 kilogram of 92 percent soy-protein isolate is about twice as much as the energy required to produce beef.

Periodical Bibliography

The following articles have been selected to supplement the diverse views presented in this chapter.

Miguel A. Altieri	"Ecological Impacts of Industrial Agriculture and the Possibility for Truly Sustainable Farming," *Monthly Review*, July/August 1998.
Dennis Avery	"The Folly of Organic Farming," *Chemistry and Industry*, December 15, 1997.
Joel Bourne	"The Organic Revolution," *Audubon*, March/April 1999.
Consumers' Research Magazine	"What Biotech Food Can Do for the Consumer: Better Food, Better Health," January 2002.
Jacques Diouf	"Like 'An Axe in the Hands of a Pathological Criminal'?" *UN Chronicle*, September/October 2001.
Mark Floegel	"The Dirt on Factory Farms," *Multinational Monitor*, August 2000.
Bernward Geier	"Will Organic Food Feed the World?" *Chemistry and Industry*, January 19, 1998.
Greenpeace	"The Food Industry's Secret Ingredient," *Greenpeace Magazine*, Winter 1999.
Brian Halweil	"The Emperor's New Crops," *World Watch*, July/August 1999.
Brian Halweil	"Organic Gold Rush," *World Watch*, May 2001.
National Cattlemen's Beef Association	"Ranching and the Environment," www.beef.org.
Laura Orlando	"McFarms Go Hog Wild," *Dollars & Sense*, July/August 1998.
Kit R. Roane	"Ripe for Abuse," *U.S. News & World Report*, April 22, 2002.
John L. Stanton	"Is Organic Produce Really Safer?" *Food Processing*, June 2001.
Dave Tilford	"Hidden Connections: Crops, Cows, Cola and the Demise of Biodiversity," *Enough!* November 26, 1999.
Paul Wymer	"Genetically Modified Food: Ambrosia or Anathema?" *Chemistry and Industry*, June 1, 1998.

CHAPTER 3

What Energy Sources Should Be Pursued?

Chapter Preface

People in China, Iceland, Japan, and New Zealand have used hot springs for cooking and bathing for hundreds of years. Ancient residents of Pompeii used geothermal water to heat buildings. For centuries, Tuscan farmers in Central Italy have grown vegetables in winter from fields heated by natural steam. Today, geothermal energy is being harnessed to run turbines, which produce electricity. Indeed, people have been utilizing geothermal energy to make life easier since human history began.

Geothermal energy originates in the molten center of the earth. Because heat travels from hot regions to colder regions, the heat produced at the earth's core eventually makes its way toward the crust, creating a temperature gradient. As water from rain and snow seeps into the earth through fissures, it eventually encounters increasingly higher temperatures and becomes steam. When this steam makes its way to the surface through cracks in the earth's crust, it appears as hot springs, geysers, mud pots, or fumaroles. However, most of the steam remains beneath the surface, a potent energy source ready to be tapped.

People today use the earth's ample geothermal reservoirs to generate electricity. In geothermal power plants, steam is pumped from the ground to turn turbine generators. There are several types of geothermal power plants, the most common being the flashed steam plant. In these facilities, hot water from wells is depressurized, which causes it to boil into steam. The steam is then used to drive a turbine generator. Dry steam plants, built where there is little groundwater, force underground steam directly into the turbine. Binary power plants use the heat from geothermal water to heat a secondary liquid, usually isobutane or isopentane, which powers the turbine generators. Binary plants can utilize cooler geothermal reservoirs because the secondary liquids vaporize at lower temperatures than water does. Hybrid power plants combine flash and binary processes.

As the population continues to grow and humanity's need for energy increases, more nations are developing their geothermal resources. As of 1999, 8,217 megawatts of electricity were being produced by over two hundred fifty geothermal power plants in twenty-two countries around the world. This energy services the needs of over 60 million people, most living in developing nations.

Geothermal electricity generation can reduce a nation's reliance on foreign sources of fossil fuels, thereby protecting it from supply disruptions caused by political unrest. In addition, geothermal energy is considered a renewable energy source, like solar and wind power, but is significantly more powerful. Marilyn L. Nemzer, Anna K. Carter, and Kenneth P. Nemzer of the Geothermal Education Office claim that "the electrical energy generated in the United States is more than twice that from solar and wind combined." Moreover, geothermal energy production does not pollute the air like the burning of fossil fuels does. According to the U.S. Department of Energy, "Electricity produced from geothermal resources in the U.S. prevents the emission of 22 million tons of carbon dioxide, 200,000 tons of sulfur dioxide, 80,000 tons of nitrogen oxides, and 110,000 tons of particulate matter every year compared to conventional coal-fired plants."

As energy demands increase worldwide, nations will increasingly look to alternative energy sources to power their economies. In the following chapter, authors discuss the merits of numerous types of energy alternatives. Utilized from the beginning of time, geothermal energy will surely be among the energy sources pursued in the years ahead.

"Photovoltaics offer a revolution in the supply of electricity."

The Use of Solar Power Should Be Increased

Martin Bond

According to Martin Bond in the following viewpoint, solar energy is showing promise of becoming an important energy alternative to fossil fuels. Bond explains that photovoltaic cells capture solar energy and transform it into electricity more cheaply than ever before. Many nations are increasing their use of solar energy, he asserts, which will reduce environmental problems produced by the burning of fossil fuels. Martin Bond, a qualified town planner, is a freelance photographer and writer.

As you read, consider the following questions:
1. What are "solar thermal power plants," as defined by the author?
2. According to Bond, how many solar roofs does the United States hope to install by 2010?
3. What are "earthships," as explained by Bond?

If Europe had a solar capital it would surely have to be Freiburg. Already one of Germany's 'greener' cities, it probably hosts more solar energy projects than anywhere else on the continent. The city even publishes a guide book illustrating examples—from solar-powered parking meters to the solar-heated headquarters of the International Solar Energy Society—and it runs to 65 pages.

Many of Freiburg's solar projects use technology perhaps more familiar to people as a power source for pocket calculators—photovoltaics, or PV for short. PV cells exploit the ability of certain metals to emit electrons when struck by light, an effect first discovered by Henri Becquerel in 1839. Consisting of thin layers of a semi-conducting material, usually silicone, a PV cell produces an electric current even when the sun is not shining—as long as there is sufficient light. With the technology being incorporated increasingly into roofs and oil walls of buildings, PV solar is fast becoming an established source of electricity.

Freiburg's success as a 'solar city' follows municipal resolutions adopted from the mid-'80s to encourage energy conservation and the use of renewable energy sources—wind, water and biomass, as well as solar. These have long been seen as a replacement for our finite supplies of fossil fuels and uranium, all of which must eventually run out. More recently, the 'renewables' have been promoted as a means of countering global warming. Substituted for fossil fuels, their use helps reduce emissions of harmful greenhouse gases.

Rise and Shining

The sun's output, though abundant and free, is also diffuse. Sceptics, especially in the electricity industry, have frequently dismissed its potential as an exploitable resource. In 1985, for example, the old Central Electricity Generating Board concluded, that: "Large-scale electricity generation from solar power has the disadvantage of high cost, large demands on land area and, for the United Kingdom (UK) low levels of solar radiation . . . Thus, for the forseeable future, this option is not attractive." According to British Nuclear Fuels, it would take "150 sq.km of solar panels" [type not specified] to produce as much energy as a typical nuclear power station. Picture the English countryside, imagine the loss of fields, hedges and farming, and the prospects for solar power might not look so sunny.

The sun's energy, however, can be harnessed in various ways. Architects have known for centuries how best to design buildings that capture and retain the sun's warmth; 'passive solar heating' as it's called is as energy-conscious as it is traditional. Solar collectors (or 'panels') can be added to buildings to heat water. There are also other methods of generating electricity, generically known as 'solar thermal' power plants. Some of these, which concentrate the sun's heat to raise steam and drive generators, undoubtedly occupy large areas of land. In the wake of the 1970's oil crises, several were built in the southwestern United States. Five are operated by the Kramer Junction Company (KJC) in California's Mojave Desert. KJC's plants comprise row upon row of parabolic trough reflectors covering a total area of more than 405 hectares. The troughs reflect the sun's rays onto a network of steel tubes containing a fluid. Heated to up to 390 [degrees] C, the fluid is pumped through heat exchangers to produce steam for electricity-generating turbines with a combined output of 150MW.

From portable indoor uses such as calculators, to generating plants alongside railways and roads, photovoltaics are adaptable, needing neither deserts nor cloudless skies. But, perhaps more importantly—in defiance of the sceptics—the application of PV systems to buildings shows that solar electricity can now be produced without needing any extra land at all.

Getting Connected

Arrays of PV modules can be designed into new buildings or added to old ones. Building-integrated PV systems have been installed on the roofs and facades of houses, factories, offices, schools, public buildings and sports stadiums. The electricity produced can be used on the spot, stored in a battery or fed to a national grid. Most systems, apart from the very smallest, are connected to local supply networks, and with suitable metering, owners can sell their surplus current to the utility.

One such system forms the roof of the home of Jeremy Leggett, a former Greenpeace scientist who now runs Solar Century, a company which designs PV systems for buildings. Leggett's roof is made of solar 'tiles' which look similar to the ordinary roof tiles they replace except that they generate electricity. "Over the past 12 months," says Leggett, "my roof has generated 14 per cent more electricity than I used, so I sold the surplus to the electricity company." Moreover, according to Solar Energy, each solar roof on an average house will, over its lifetime, prevent 34 tons of greenhouse gas emissions.

Hitting the Roof

The energy potential of light falling on buildings is enormous. A 1999 report for the Department of Trade and Industry shows that PV systems installed on "all available domestic and non-domestic buildings" in the UK by 2025 could generate almost as much electricity as the average we consume over a year.

BP Amoco, an oil company also aiming to be one of the world's largest manufacturers of photovoltaic cells, claims that "if every south-facing roof and office wall in the UK were clad with solar panels, the sun's energy could generate more than the UK's complete electricity requirement." In practice, a country like Britain, with its ever-changing weather and seasonal variations, would not be expected to rely entirely on photovoltaics for power. But such calculations suggest that solar energy, especially if complemented by other renewables, could play a far more important role than previously thought.

Several countries have launched remarkably ambitious plans for solar electricity. In Europe, Germany was first in 1990 with its '1,000 Roofs Programme.' This joint initiative by the federal and state governments invited applications for roof-mounted grid-connected PV systems with outputs in the range of 1–5 kWp, typically suitable for houses. Installation costs would be offset by 70 per cent subsidies. After initial enquiries from 60,000 households, 2,250 systems were eventually approved. The German target has since been increased to 100,000 roofs, equivalent to 300 MWp of electricity. Switzerland has been another pioneer, with some PV projects sited high in the Alps—proof that cold weather is no deterrent to solar electricity. Italy has a 10,000 PV roof programme, while the Dutch government is aiming for 100,000 PV roofs by 2010, rising to 560,000 by 2020.

Further targets have been set by the European Commission. A 1997 Commission White Paper proposed a "campaign for take-off" to generate 12 per cent of the EU's [European Union's] electricity from renewable sources by 2010. In addition to 40,000 MW of wind farms and 10,000 MWth biomass, the commission aims to promote the installation of 500,000 PV systems on roofs and facades by that date. A parallel initiative proposes to export another 500,000 PV systems to villages outside the EU. These 'solar village' schemes are intended to kick start decentralised electrification in developing countries, while boosting the solar manufacturing industry and jobs in Europe.

Time to Embrace Solar Power

The public recognizes, now more than ever, that it is time to embrace renewable technologies. A *Newsweek* poll recorded that 84 percent of Americans desire more federal investment in solar and wind energy. In November 2001, 73 percent of voters in San Francisco supported a $100 million bond to place solar on buildings in their city. The Sacramento Municipal Utility District (SMUD) has a waiting list of people who wish to install solar on their rooftops and has placed over 10 MW of systems in service. Home builders are partnering with companies in making solar a standard feature. In certain locations in California, Home Depot is selling complete solar energy systems. This demand will spread.

Glenn Hamer, *World & I*, June 2002.

Outside Europe, Japan is subsidising 10,000 PV installations on domestic buildings, while the United States eclipses everyone with the ambitious goal of one million solar roofs by 2010, although this includes solar thermal systems (solar panels) as well as photovoltaics.

Absent from this burgeoning list is any comparable programme in Britain. Following the European Commission's proposals, a UK government-funded task force, including representatives from Solar Century, BP Solar and several financial institutions, recommended a UK programme of at least 70,000 PV rooftops, a national share of the EU target. Yet despite the government's own 'renewables' obligation'—to obtain five per cent of electricity from renewable sources by 2003, and ten per cent by 2010—the task force's recommendations have been ignored.

Thus, at the dawn of the 21st century, there were still less than 100 building-integrated PV systems in Britain. Financial support from the government for actual projects is limited to a proposed 'field trial' of PV systems on 100 houses; five or six large-scale 'showcase' PV building projects per year, and the Scolar educational project. The latter involves installing 100 'canopies' incorporating PV cells, and monitoring equipment, at selected schools and colleges.

Golden Opportunities

Notwithstanding the massive house-building programme anticipated over the next few years—a golden opportunity to ensure that new buildings contribute to sustainable development rather than global warming—it seems that the solar millenium beginning in other countries is being largely ignored in Britain, a situation that exasperates the renewable energy community. Many point a finger at the Department of Trade and Industry (DTI), home to a cautious bureaucracy, resistant to new ideas, and associated with powerful vested interests, especially in the non-renewable electricity industry.

For Jeremy Leggett, "solar PV is a classic disruptive technology, poised on the edge of a trillion dollar market." That shining opportunity is apparent even to the oil companies. Recognising that their traditional product will not last for ever, some are diversifying into renewables and with highly optimistic expectations. Shell, for example, which now manufactures PV cells in Germany and the Netherlands, predicts that: "In 2050, half the world could be powered by renewable energy." BP Amoco, who, like Shell, has been installing PV cells on some of its filling stations, reckons that "by the year 2050 the whole of Europe's electrical requirements could be met by solar power."

The key, though, is a reduction of costs. Although the price of PV cells has fallen considerably, PV electricity from building systems is still uncompetitive without subsidy against other sources of electricity. As more PV systems are installed, a market evolution could result in solar electricity becoming truly competitive.

SELFless Energy

There are more than two billion people without access to electricity, according to the United Nations Development Programme. While the rest of us are able to log-on to the internet to obtain information or exchange emails, when night falls in the developing world 70 per cent of the people cannot even turn on a light bulb. Most of these 'unelectrified' people live in rural areas that have little chance of being connected to a fossil-fuel powered national utility grid. This is where the Solar Electric Light Fund (SELF) steps in. A non-profit charitable organisation founded in 1990, SELF promotes and develops energy self-sufficiency in developing countries. Using the latest photovoltaic (PV) technology, its mission is to bring the developing world out of the darkness without generating more greenhouse gases.

SELF also seeks to remedy the environmental consequence of urban migration as people leave rural communities, putting pressure on already overcrowded towns and cities. SELF's list of achievements to date include: operating a rural solar enterprise in Karnataka, India; helping to design and prepare the first PV project for the Global Environment Facility aimed at electrifying up to 10,000 houses in Zimbabwe; and equipping a rural school in South Africa with solar-powered computers and wireless internet access. Go to www.self.org for more information.

A Shining Example

Photovoltaics offer a revolution in the supply of electricity. Add a storage system such as batteries, and those idealistic dreams of energy self-sufficiency can be lived for real. In the American southwest this is happening already. The Taos area of New Mexico is home to the 'earthship' concept, designed by Michael Reynolds of Solar Survival Architecture. Earthship houses combine elements of traditional adobe design with walls built from discarded vehicle tyres, cans and earth—re-using society's garbage is an important part of the concept. Earthships collect and recycle their own water and waste and generate electricity from PV cells. On the high desert plateau of New Mexico, they evoke native American pueblos crossed with something you might find on the moon.

In fact, the earthships built so far are not entirely self-sufficient. Although independent of utility services and with ample solar electricity, most people buy propane for cooking. But energy is only a part of the project, which addresses the wider issues of a sustainable lifestyle: "The earthship concept is a method of creating a fertile soil from which a community can grow," writes Reynolds. Two earthship colonies have already been started in the foothills of the nearby Sangre de Cristo mountains and designs exist for whole cities of earthship buildings.

"For all of solar's many positive attributes, the problems of harnessing its power remain."

Solar Power Is Not a Viable Energy Source

William Booth

Generating electricity from the sun remains inefficient and expensive, according to William Booth in the following viewpoint. Booth argues that despite generous government subsidies, solar panels are still too expensive for the average homeowner to purchase. In addition, photovoltaic technology is still in its infancy, as evidenced by the limited amount of energy that solar panels capture and convert for household use, he asserts. Booth claims that many logistical problems have dampened solar energy's appeal as well, including the difficulty of finding reputable contractors to install solar panels. William Booth is a staff writer for the *Washington Post*.

As you read, consider the following questions:

1. According to Booth, how much does a photovoltaic package cost?
2. How many solar energy systems have been installed in California, as reported by the author?
3. As stated by Booth, what happens to a solar-powered home during a blackout?

In 2000, Los Angeles, California, announced its intent to become "the Solar Capital of the World," with 100,000 roofs covered with solar electric panels by the end of the decade, an audacious goal to transform the homes of this smoggy but sunny metropolis into miniature power plants.

To fulfill what is perhaps the nation's most ambitious solar campaign, the Los Angeles Department of Water and Power began offering substantial "buy down" subsidies that would reimburse rate payers for half the price of each new solar energy system. For the average home, a photovoltaic package costs between $10,000 and $20,000, parts and labor included, before the rebate.

How many have been installed [in the year following the announcement]?

At last count, about 40.

That leaves only 99,960 rooftops to go.

The George W. Bush administration, and especially Vice President Dick Cheney, architect of its energy plan, have been criticized for skepticism regarding alternative energy sources. But a close examination of the Los Angeles solar experiment and a review of similar programs suggest the former oilmen in the White House have a point: Solar, at least, has not proven ready for prime time.

The Problems of Harnessing the Sun's Energy

For all of Los Angeles's good intentions, and for all of solar's many positive attributes, the problems of harnessing its power remain. Some of those challenges are economic and some technological; others are more mundane, but often ignored, such as finding a qualified contractor a homeowner can trust to drill dozens of holes in the roofs to mount the things.

In a reprise of the 1980s, solar again is hot. The price of photovoltaics is dropping and interest is growing. Other states such as New York, Arizona, Florida and Washington are moving to join California in major efforts to wire homes to draw power from the sun.

But as many Americans are beginning to understand, the delivery of energy is like a complex, interconnected assembly line, and the devil lurks in the details.

The Los Angeles experiment tells the story shared by other

locales. In L.A., for example, the city's lone solar panel manufacturer has not been able to supply enough systems to meet demand.

The systems, too, are often oversold by solar proponents. In the real world, most do not pay for themselves in a few years, as some advocates claim, but take 20 years or more to return their initial cost in the form of reduced utility bills.

Nor are the systems maintenance-free: At a minimum, the rooftop panels must be routinely cleaned of pollution, dust and leaves.

They cannot be installed efficiently on homes without shade-free, south-facing roofs; the shadow from a neighbor's palm tree can frustrate the system's photovoltaic cells.

Nor will the most common systems allow buyers to live "off the grid," unless they want to purchase a large bank of batteries. Even with the batteries, homeowners probably would not be able to run their washing machines and air conditioners at the same time.

"It is not an economic proposition at this point," concedes Terry Peterson, a solar expert at Electric Power Research Institute in Palo Alto, California. But one day, Peterson predicts, 100 years from now, solar energy will provide a substantial percentage of the world's energy needs. In a decade or two, the cost of solar will likely be competitive with other energy sources such as natural gas, nuclear or coal.

But now? It is still a luxury item. "Like buying a swimming pool," Peterson says.

"I really like the idea of running my house with solar power," says Andrew Chin, a potential customer in Los Angeles who has been researching a purchase. "But they're still pretty expensive, even with the rebates, and so I gotta ask myself, what am I doing this for," his conscience or his wallet. "I'm thinking I might wait until they work the kinks out."

The Coming Age of Solar Energy

The most knowledgeable and experienced solar contractor in Los Angeles is probably Graham Owen, the founder, owner and single full-time employee of Go Solar Co.

His installation of a one-kilowatt solar electric system on a home in the San Fernando Valley was the first to be awarded a rebate by the Los Angeles power department in March, 2001.

How many systems has he installed as part of the rebate program? Three.

But Owen is a true believer, and over the next year, he plans to cover hundreds of roofs with solar panels. On his shelf, Owen still has an unreturned library book, "The Coming Age of Solar Energy," published in 1963, and checked out from his high school in Lennox Hills, Illinois, in 1979. "I guess we're still stuck in the coming age of solar energy," he says, smiling. He recalls that the buzz about solar water heaters in the 1980s led to disappointment with shoddy workmanship and less than spectacular energy savings.

Hopelessly Ineffective

All of America's central station solar electricity is generated in California. At maximum capacity, California's nine solar stations—with a combined total of 11 square miles of mirrors focused on steam drums that drive steam turbines—can generate 413 megawatts (MW) of electricity, 0.8% of the state's capacity. Because the sun sets at night and is sometimes attenuated by clouds, these plants produce only 0.3% of California's electricity. They owe their economic existence to federal solar power tax credits awarded on top of California's inflated Public Utilities Regulatory Policy Act (PURPA) contracts and renewable power subsidies. When these tax credits were interrupted for eleven months in 1991, the plants' operator, LUZ, immediately went bankrupt. Today SEGS, an Israeli government corporation, operates them at a loss. . . .

After two decades of subsidized development, [solar power] remains hopelessly ineffective.

Jack Wakeland, *The Intellectual Activist*, August 2001.

Until recently, there has been little widespread interest in solar electric power. Since 1998, the California Energy Commission has been pushing its own program to encourage homeowners to erect photovoltaic panels on their roofs, offering to subsidize about one-third of the cost.

Across a state with a population of about 35 million, only 450 solar energy systems have been installed on homes.

Then the 2000 California energy crisis struck, with its

power interruptions and steep rate increases, and the phone calls began to overwhelm Owen's voice mail.

"On days with rolling blackouts? I get a hundred calls, maybe more," Owen says. His Web site, *www.solarexpert.com* is now receiving 3,000 hits a day. Customers are begging him to do jobs.

The Los Angeles power department reports a similar surge in interest since the energy crisis began. "Customer demand has shot through the roof," says Angelina Galiteva, executive director for strategic planning at the Department of Water and Power. She estimates that her department receives 1,000 calls on some days about its solar subsidy program.

Yet while the reliability and cost of solar electric technologies continue to improve, solar power today accounts for only a sliver of the national pie chart of energy production—less than 1 percent. The country produces about 300 megawatts of electricity with solar—about the same amount produced by a single mid-sized traditional power plant.

The current trend for photovoltaics is not to erect large centralized solar farms in the desert, an experiment that withered in the 1980s, but to pursue "distributed generation" or individual units on scattered rooftops.

The problem has consistently been the cost of the solar panels, which has been too steep to justify them, except for customers who are committed environmentalists or techies who like the elegance of the systems.

Making It Pay

Los Angeles began its solar experiment after [state] legislators mandated that utilities spend about 3 percent of their revenue on efficiency, conservation and renewable energy. For solar, the power department committed $75 million over the next five years—enough to subsidize panels on 7,500 homes.

The power department will pay $5 for each watt of solar installed on a residence or business. Homeowners typically purchase a one-kilowatt or two-kilowatt (1,000 or 2,000 watts, respectively) solar electric system, meaning that the municipal utility would pay between $5,000 and $10,000 of the cost up front—an enticing, tax-free offer.

"For many years, I wanted to do solar, but it was so expensive," says LaWanda Geary in the San Fernando Valley, who had Owen install 32 panels for a two-kilowatt system on her sunny roof. "The rebate really got me going. I don't know many times when the government offers to pay half of anything."

The systems that are eligible for rebates must be tied into a utility's electric power grid, meaning that during the day, when the sun is shining, the panels are adding a stream of electrons used by the home to run its lights and appliances.

If there is a surplus of solar power, that electricity goes back into the power lines and is passed along to a neighbor, and the electric meter at the house actually runs backward. On cloudy days, and at night, the home is not being powered by solar energy, but getting its electricity the traditional way from the power lines.

Calculations on savings vary. A two-kilowatt solar system can supply an average-sized home with 20 to 80 percent of its electrical needs, depending on how many lights, appliances and air conditioners are running, and how efficient they are.

After the subsidy, and depending on how the system is paid for (in cash or with borrowed funds), a solar system can pay for itself in as little as six years and as much as 36 years. Owen assumes about 20 years.

Potential solar clients, moreover, often mistakenly assume that going with the sun will take them off the grid, which is not possible without a large bank of batteries that costs several thousand dollars more. Because the solar panels are still wired to the power grid, if there is a blackout, the power in a solar house goes off, just like everyone else's. If uninterrupted power is needed, Owen suggests a diesel generator.

Logistical Concerns

Galiteva does cite one real advantage of solar: It reduces the electricity that must be purchased from power companies and protects, to some degree, a solar home from the full brunt of upwardly spiraling rate increases. Unfortunately for solar enthusiasts, the L.A. Department of Water and Power, which was not deregulated along with the three other major utilities in California, has perhaps the cheapest and most stable supply of electricity in the state, making the economic argument harder to make.

To receive the full $5 per watt subsidy, the L.A. Department of Water and Power requires a homeowner to purchase solar panels from a manufacturer based in the city. The idea is not only to become the solar capital of the world but also to encourage local growth of an emerging industry and create jobs.

One hitch is that no solar panel makers were located in Los Angeles.

After lengthy negotiations, Siemens Solar Industries, based in Camarillo, California, an hour's drive to the north, announced in February 2001 that it would open a solar panel manufacturing plant in Los Angeles. But it is not a complete facility: The L.A. plant does only some final assembly and then the units must be returned to Camarillo for final testing and shipping.

Tina Nickerson, a spokeswoman for Siemens Solar, estimates her company has sold "a couple dozen" to L.A. homeowners for the rebate program. But she, too, reports that the interest from consumers is sometimes overwhelming and that supply has been a problem. Most U.S.-manufactured units are shipped overseas to places such as Germany, Japan and Scandinavia, which have had generous subsidies in place for years.

LaWanda Geary had to call Siemens herself to push them to deliver panels for her house—and she was eligible for the rebate because of a stopgap compromise that allows Siemens to ship solar panels from Camarillo until its L.A. plant is fully operational.

Everyone involved concedes there have been bottlenecks. Siemens now says it has enough panels to begin to meet demand, and Owen and the city are hoping things will sort themselves out, especially if more solar manufacturers are drawn to Los Angeles. But proponents worry about what will happen when the subsidies run out.

"Selling solar is now the easy part," Owen says, "I could sell a hundred a week. It's getting them up on the roof that's the hard part."

"Nuclear power . . . provides a viable and safe means for satisfying our growing need for electricity."

The Use of Nuclear Power Should Be Increased

Douglas S. McGregor

Douglas S. McGregor asserts in the following viewpoint that nuclear power is a safe way to produce electricity. He claims that highly publicized nuclear accidents such as those that occurred at Chernobyl and Three Mile Island were anomalies. In fact, he contends, nuclear power plants have safety measures in place to prevent any serious radiation leaks or explosions from occurring. Moreover, the small amount of radioactive waste produced by nuclear reactors is safely contained within the plant itself, he maintains. Douglas S. McGregor is the director of the Semiconductor Materials and Radiological Technologies Laboratory at the University of Michigan at Ann Arbor.

As you read, consider the following questions:
1. What emissions do nuclear power plants produce, according to McGregor?
2. As stated by the author, how many years would a person have to live near a nuclear power plant to receive the same amount of radiation that he or she would get from a single diagnostic X ray?
3. Why would an accident such as the one that occurred at the Chernobyl plant never take place at a Western nuclear power plant, in the author's opinion?

The rolling blackouts that occurred in California, and the threat of power shortages elsewhere, should focus national attention on a viable energy option that is now responsible for about 20 percent of our electrical power generation, yet could easily be responsible for much more. In fact, France now uses this energy option to generate nearly 80 percent of its electricity, and a number of other countries are also more dependent on this energy option than is the United States (see Figure 1). Ironically, the technology in question was invented and developed here.

A Safer Alternative

We are referring, of course, to nuclear power. This industry has been brought to a virtual standstill in this country based on fears that nuclear power is far too dangerous to use. Those fears are unfounded, however, and America should take a second look at this amazing form of power generation. France, Belgium, Switzerland, and other countries that generate a higher percentage of their electrical output via nuclear power than does the United States have been able to do so without loss of life and without harming the environment. Why should it be any different here?

This is not to say that nuclear power is 100 percent safe. (No form of power generation is perfectly safe.) Nuclear power is simply safer than other alternatives for generating large amounts of electrical energy, such as oil or coal plants. This is true, in part, because the fuel in a nuclear power plant is highly concentrated. One uranium fuel pellet—typically measuring about 0.3-inch diameter by 0.5-inch long—can produce the equivalent energy of 17,000 cubic feet of natural gas, 1,780 pounds of coal, or 149 gallons of oil. Because relatively little fuel is used, relatively little waste is produced.

Moreover, the waste that is produced in a nuclear power plant is contained within the plant itself, where it can eventually be removed for long-term storage. This is not the case with fossil fuel plants, which emit tons of pollutants through their smokestacks into the atmosphere. Nuclear plants do not emit pollutants into the air and for that reason they do not have smokestacks. Some nuclear power plants have cooling towers that are sometimes mistaken for smokestacks, but those cooling towers emit water vapor.

Interestingly, an article that appeared in the January-February 2000 issue of *Foreign Affairs*, entitled "The Need for Nuclear Power," also concludes that fossil fuel electrical power plants are actually more hazardous to people than nuclear power plants. That conclusion, in that source, is particularly notable since *Foreign Affairs* is the journal of the Council on Foreign Relations (CFR), and the CFR is a promoter of internationalism as opposed to American independence. Yet the nuclear power option could make the U.S. less dependent on foreign oil.

Written by Richard Rhodes and Denis Beller (neither of whom, by the way, is a member of the CFR), the *Foreign Affairs* article notes that pollutants from coal-burning plants cause an estimated 15,000 premature deaths in the United States *every year*. In fact, write Rhodes and Beller, "A 1,000-megawatt-electric (MWe) coal-fired power plant releases about 100 times as much radioactivity into the environment as a comparable nuclear plant." Moreover, they explain:

> Running a 1,000-MWe power plant for a year requires 2,000 train cars of coal or 10 supertankers of oil but only 12 cubic meters of natural uranium. Out of the other end of fossil-fuel plants . . . come thousands of tonnes of noxious gases, particulates, and heavy-metal-bearing (and radioactive) ash, plus solid hazardous waste—up to 500,000 tonnes of sulfur from coal, more than 300,000 tonnes from oil, and 200,000 tonnes from natural gas. In contrast, a 1,000 MWe nuclear plant releases no noxious gases or other pollutants and much less radioactivity per capita than is encountered from airline travel, a home smoke detector, or a television set.

What Are the Risks?

Arguments against nuclear power reactors generally revolve around three main issues: nuclear waste; plutonium build-up; and radioactivity. Each of these issues is addressed below:

• *Nuclear waste:* Reactor fuel consists of uranium that has been formed into a usable metal alloy and produced as small pellets, rods, or plates. The fuel is encapsulated with a metal cladding, such as zircaloy, to provide mechanical strength and to prevent inadvertent outside radioactive contamination. Nuclear reactor waste or spent nuclear fuel consists of the fuel pellets that have been used in a reactor for a long period of time (usually several years) and have lost their ability to efficiently release energy. The spent fuel has many radioactive byproducts, such as the fission fragments, and must be stored to prevent hazardous exposure.

Presently, spent fuel is stored in shielded basins of water or dry storage vaults at the nuclear power plants. The radioactive by-products must be allowed to decay to safe levels, which will take hundreds to thousands of years. Solid nuclear waste containers are designed, through both natural and engineered safety barriers, to withstand underground storage for at least 10,000 years.

Figure 1: Dependency on Nuclear Power Plants for Various Industrialized Nations (1999)

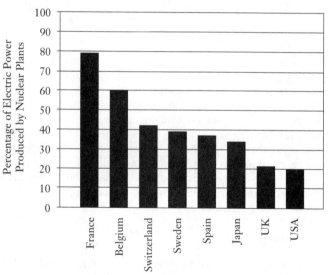

Richard Rhodes and Denis Beller, "The Need for Nuclear Power," *Foreign Affairs*, January/February 2000.

Spent fuel can be safely stored on a permanent basis once a national repository is finally approved. Planned nuclear waste storage facilities such as the Yucca Mountain site are still undergoing environmental impact studies, having suffered numerous delays for the opening date. At present the opening of a national repository for the long-term storage of nuclear waste is over 12 years behind schedule, and at least one government laboratory source (see http://nsnfp.inel.gov) states that a national repository may not be available for another 20 years. But the problem is political, not scientific.

One way to address the nuclear waste issue is to reduce the amount of waste that needs to be stored. Other countries, such as France, have progressive nuclear fuel recycling programs whereby a large percentage of the unused uranium (and the small amount of plutonium produced) in the spent fuel is salvaged and then processed into new reactor fuel. According to the Nuclear Energy Institute (NEI), only 3 percent of spent fuel is actual fission byproduct waste; 96 percent is unused uranium, and the remaining 1 percent is the unused plutonium created during the fuel cycle. The benefits of spent nuclear fuel recycling include more efficient nuclear fuel usage, reduced chance of nuclear materials proliferation, and less buildup of nuclear reactor waste byproducts. The benefits of making more efficient use of nuclear fuel are obvious, yet the United States does not have a nuclear fuel recycling program in place at this time.

• *Plutonium build-up:* Western nuclear power reactors are constructed and engineered in a manner that minimizes plutonium build-up, and much of the plutonium that is produced inside the reactor is used during an ordinary fuel cycle. Moreover, it should be kept in mind that using fissile material for reactor fuel is a far better method of preventing nuclear proliferation than storage or burying those materials. After the fissile material has been used as nuclear fuel, it cannot possibly be used for weapons, thereby eliminating the possibility of use by potential terrorists.

• *Radiation:* The amount of radiation that is emitted by nuclear power plants, as already indicated, is minuscule. According to Environmental Protection Agency (EPA) guidelines, the annual whole body dose to the public is limited to 25 millirems for uranium fuel cycle operations.

But before anyone panics at such a generous regulatory allotment, let's put into proper focus how much radiation a millirem is. According to information from the NEI, the National Council on Radiation Protection and Measurements (NCRP), and the EPA, natural background radiation from the Earth's crust ranges from 23 millirems per year at the Atlantic Coast to 90 millirems per year on the Colorado Plateau. Radiation *inside* the body is approximately 40 millirems per year from the food and water we consume and up to 200 millirems per year from natural levels of radon in the air we breathe. The annual radiation dose reaching us from outer space ranges from 26 millirems at sea level to 53 millirems at elevations between 7,000–8,000 feet. The radiation dose from a simple medical X-ray is approximately 20 millirems, and the average radiation dose from a 1,000-mile airline flight is about 1 millirem—meaning that a traveler who flies across the country and back will accumulate about 5 millirems. We also receive 1–2 millirems annually from watching television and would receive another 7 millirems annually from living in a brick building.

Now consider this: We would receive .03 millirem annually by living within a 50-mile radius of a coal-fired power plant, but *only .009 millirem by living within a 50-mile radius of a nuclear power plant!* Incredible as it may seem, we would have to live near a nuclear power plant for more than 2,000 years in order to receive the same amount of radiation that we would get from a single diagnostic medical X-ray.

Anti-nuclear propaganda notwithstanding, there is nothing unnatural about radioactivity, radioactive elements, or even nuclear reactors. In fact, all three have existed in nature without any help from man and continue to exist today. At least 14 naturally occurring fission reactors have been documented in the Oklo-Okélobondo natural geological uranium formation in Gabon, a country on the west coast of Africa. These "fossil reactors" contained sufficient concentrations of U-235 for the chain reactions to occur, and those reactions were not regulated by control rods or any other form of human intervention. The discovery of these natural reactors clearly discredits the anti-nuclear, alarmist claim that man is somehow tampering with nature by building nuclear power plants.

Nuclear power plants are based on multiple layers of defense designed to protect the environment from the radioactive material inside the reactor core. But what happens if something goes wrong—so terribly wrong that those layers of defense are breached? What then?

The most serious accident possible is the release of radioactive material into the environment. It is not a nuclear explosion, for the simple reason that the uranium fuel used in a nuclear power plant does not contain a high enough concentration of U-235 to make a nuclear explosion even theoretically possible. To make such an explosion possible, the uranium fuel inside a reactor would have to be enriched to about 90 percent U-235, but it is only enriched to about 3.5 percent.

The worst nuclear power plant disaster in history occurred when the Chernobyl reactor in the Ukraine experienced a heat (and gas)—*not* nuclear—explosion. If such an explosion were to have occurred in a Western nuclear power plant, the explosion would have been contained because *all* Western plants are required to have a containment building—a solid structure of steel-reinforced concrete that completely encapsulates the nuclear reactor vessel. The Chernobyl plant did not have this fundamental safety structure, and so the explosion blew the top of the reactor building off, spewing radiation and reactor core pieces into the air.

But the design of the Chernobyl plant was inferior in other ways as well. Unlike the Chernobyl reactor, Western power plant nuclear reactors are designed, under operating conditions, to have negative power coefficients of reactivity that make such runaway accidents impossible. The bottom line is that the flawed Chernobyl nuclear power plant would never have been licensed to operate in the U.S. or any other Western country, and the accident that occurred there simply would not occur in a Western nuclear power plant.

The circumstances surrounding the Chernobyl accident were in many ways the worst possible, with an exposed reactor core and an open building. Thirty-one plant workers and firemen died directly from radiation exposure at Chernobyl. Also, it is projected that over 3,400 local residents will eventually acquire and die of cancer due to their exposure to the radioactive fallout. By comparison, within a matter of hours more than 2,300 were killed and as many as 200,000 others injured in a non-nuclear accident when a toxic gas cloud escaped from the Union Carbide pesticide plant in Bhopal, India.

According to conventional wisdom, the worst nuclear power accident in this country occurred at the Three Mile Island plant in Pennsylvania. Yet, in that incident, nobody was killed and nobody was injured.

Deadly Environmentalists

One exception, perhaps, could be Dr. Edward Teller, the distinguished pro-nuclear physicist who played a key role in the development of nuclear advancements during and after World War II. In a two-page ad appearing in the *Wall Street Journal* for July 31, 1979, Dr. Teller explained that, at 71 years of age and working 20 hours per day, the strain of refuting some of the anti-nuclear "propaganda that [activist] Ralph Nader, [actress] Jane Fonda and their ilk" were "spewing to the news media" in the wake of Three Mile Island led to a heart attack. He continued: "You might say that I was the only one whose health was affected by that reactor near Harrisburg. No, that would be wrong. It was not the reactor. It was Jane Fonda. Reactors are not dangerous."

The event at Three Mile Island occurred from faulty instrumentation that gave erroneous readings for the reactor vessel environment. Due to a series of equipment failures and human errors, plus inadequate instrumentation, the reactor core was compromised and underwent a partial melt. Yet radioactive water released from the core configuration was safely confined within the containment building structure, and very little radiation was released into the environment.

The Three Mile Island incident actually underscores the relative safety of nuclear power plants since the safety devices *worked* as designed and *prevented* any injury from occurring to humans, animals, or the environment. Moreover, the accident directly resulted in improved procedures, instrumentation, and safety systems, and now our nuclear reactor power plants are substantially safer. The Three Mile Island Unit 2 core has been cleaned up and the radioactive deposit properly stored; Three Mile Island Unit 1 is still operating with an impeccable record.

Status of the Nuclear Industry

There are now 104 operating nuclear power units in this country that are responsible for about 20 percent of our total electrical generation. By comparison, over half our electricity is generated by coal-burning plants.

Our nuclear power plants have not only been generating electricity safely, they also have been doing so economically. The February 2001 issue of *Nuclear Energy Insight* listed the average nuclear energy production cost for 1999 as 1.83 cents per kW-hour, as compared to 3.18 cents/kW-hr for oil-burning plants, 3.52 cents per kW-hr for natural gas plants, and 2.07 cents per kW-hr for coal plants. . . .

For too long the nuclear industry has been a victim of scare tactics and outrageously false propaganda. Yet truth is a much more potent weapon than falsehood, and the truth about nuclear power is that it provides a viable and safe means for satisfying our growing need for electricity. The looming specter of a severe energy shortage in this country should spark an increasing demand for nuclear power on the part of Americans who don't want to be left in the dark. And that, of course, will create a growing problem for the radical environmental lobby that is not only anti-nuclear power but anti-development.

4

"*Clusters of cancers, birth defects and various immune disorders have been reported in [communities surrounding nuclear power plants].*"

Nuclear Power Is Dangerous and Expensive

Karen Charman

In the following viewpoint, Karen Charman contends that nuclear energy is expensive, damaging to the environment, and dangerous to human health. According to Charman, when including the costs of building plants and dealing with nuclear waste, nuclear power is far more expensive than its proponents claim. She also maintains that nuclear power is not the environmentally friendly energy source that many in the media contend; in fact, nuclear power generation emits gases that harm the ozone layer. In addition, Charman argues, radioactive waste and gases produced by nuclear power plants increase the incidence of cancer, birth defects, and immune system disorders in surrounding communities. Karen Charman is a New York–based investigative journalist specializing in environmental and health reporting.

As you read, consider the following questions:

1. What events contributed to Americans' fear of nuclear power, as reported by Charman?
2. Why are many estimates of the costs of nuclear power production inaccurate, in Charman's opinion?
3. Why does the author consider Yucca Mountain an unsuitable site for storing nuclear waste?

Karen Charman, "Nuclear Power Gets Media Makeover," *Extra!*, July/August 2001, pp. 23–25. Copyright © 2001 by *Extra!* Reproduced by permission.

"Nuclear Follies," a February 11, 1985 cover story in *Forbes*, declared U.S. nuclear power "the largest managerial disaster in business history." With $125 billion invested, the magazine wrote, "only the blind, or the biased, can now think that most of the money has been well spent. It is a defeat for the U.S. consumer and for the competitiveness of U.S. industry, for the utilities that undertook the program and for the private enterprise system that made it possible."

Pretty strong words. But now, a mere 16 years later, nuclear power is being widely reported in the mainstream media as not only the cheapest source of electricity, but also as a clean and environmentally friendly form of energy that we now must embrace to combat global warming.

Even before the 1979 partial meltdown at Three Mile Island [nuclear power plant in Pennsylvania], electric utilities that had bought into the nuclear option on the promise that it would be "too cheap to meter" had begun racking up huge debts because the technology turned out to be vastly more expensive and complicated than they had anticipated. After the accident, and the increased public and press scrutiny that resulted, the industry was forced to adopt costly new safety modifications.

Then, in April 1986, a catastrophic meltdown occurred at Chernobyl [nuclear power plant in the former Soviet Union], spewing high levels of radiation across Europe and galvanizing public opposition to nuclear power both here and in Western Europe. In the U.S., a total of 117 nuclear reactors were eventually canceled, says Safe Energy Communication Council executive director Scott Denman—pointing out that the cancellations outnumber the country's 103 currently operating reactors.

Except for one or two plants that came online in the mid-'90s, no others were scheduled. "As we went through the '90s, all those reporters who had been focused on safety issues after Three Mile Island, then the cost, and then safety issues again after Chernobyl, began to drift away," Denman says. "As events in the industry quieted down, so did the regional reporting, and nuclear power faded from public view," he explains. The consequence is the recent wave of largely uncritical and shallow reporting.

Nuclear's New Day

Until the George W. Bush administration took office, any public discussion of expanding nuclear power might have been dismissed as wishful thinking on the nuclear industry's part. True, the industry has dreamed of its comeback for many years. But it wasn't until the energy fiasco erupted in California,[1] and the Bush administration and other pro-nuclear politicians began calling for massive increases in energy production, that a nuclear power renaissance could be considered.

Now that nukes are on the table again, many of the "facts" the corporate media are dishing up seem to have come straight from the Nuclear Energy Institute (NEI), the industry's main lobbying group. Take claims about the cost of nuclear power. *ABC World News Tonight* informed its viewers (1/6/01) that nuclear production costs are "lower than any other source, even coal." This claim was echoed by NBC (3/19/01), whose parent company, General Electric, is one of the largest nuclear power plant designers. In comparing the costs of nuclear power to other sources, the *Houston Chronicle* (4/17/01) even used figures that came from an NEI press release—1.83 cents per kilowatt hour for nuclear, 2.07 cents for coal, 3.52 cents for natural gas—without citing the source. Even *Popular Science* (5/01) reported that the inherent instability of fossil fuel costs "has created a long-awaited opening for the oft-despised but super-cheap (less than 2 cents per kilowatt-hour) nuclear."

These figures, however, include only the operating costs of running the reactors. The big ticket costs associated with nuclear power have been shifted onto the public. In virtually all cases, ratepayers and taxpayers have been saddled with the capital costs of building nuclear plants, which in some cases exceeded $10 billion apiece. In total, about $300 billion (in 2001 dollars) has been spent on nuclear plants, according to Charles Komanoff, an economist who researches nuclear power.

The public also picks up the tab for dealing with the reactors' deadly radioactive waste, which the Department of

---

1. In 2000, California suffered numerous blackouts due to temporary energy shortages.

Energy most recently estimated at $58 billion. The cost of "decommissioning"—tearing down and cleaning up old, contaminated nukes once they wear out—also falls to us. As an indication of this bill, decommissioning the Yankee Rowe plant in Massachusetts, which is about one-seventh the size of the largest nuclear reactor now operating, is expected to cost almost $500 million, says Paul Gunter, director of the reactor project at the Nuclear Information & Resource Service, a watchdog group.

On top of all that, nuclear utilities evade the lion's share of the cost of a potential nuclear disaster. Under the federal Price-Anderson Act, originally passed in 1957 . . . , a utility's liability for an accident is limited to $7 billion. Current estimates of Chernobyl's costs, by comparison, exceed $350 billion.

Sweep It Under the Mountain

In the 1950s, the federal government pledged that the public would inherit the nuclear industry's so-called "high-level waste" or "spent fuel"; the mildly radioactive uranium fuel originally loaded into the reactor core comes out 2.5 million times more radioactive. A Nevada state agency report put the toxicity in perspective: A spent fuel assembly out of the reactor core for 10 years would emit enough radiation to kill somebody standing three feet from it in less than three minutes. The public has already spent more than $6 billion on high-level waste disposal, though no long-term storage system has yet been devised.

Spent fuel remains deadly for at least tens of thousands of years. In order to keep it isolated from the environment, nuclear planners came up with the idea of burying it deep underground. Only one site, Nevada's Yucca Mountain, is currently under consideration, and the Department of Energy (DOE) is expected to rule on its suitability later in 2001.[2]

Nuclear proponents claim that once there is a place to take the waste, the waste problem is solved. Only "politics" is standing in the way, they say. The *Christian Science Moni-*

2. The viability of Yucca Mountain as a hazardous waste storage site is still being debated.

tor (1/22/01)—which erroneously placed Yucca Mountain in Arizona—quoted the Nuclear Energy Institute's Martin Fertel saying: "We want politics to be moved aside and let science, the data, and the regulatory process go forward." The *Monitor* follows Fertel's comment, writing: "Many in the industry suspect that the Clinton administration blocked action on this crucial site for political reasons—to win electoral support in Arizona."

Risk and Liability

Unhappy experience has improved the nuclear industry's practices. Yet plant operators still insist on having in place a federal law called the Price-Anderson Act. It says that above the modest limit of its operators' pool and government insurance for small nuclear-power disasters, nobody is liable for a large one: If another Chernobyl [nuclear disaster] harms you or your property, it's your problem. Nuclear disasters also are excluded from ordinary insurance policies. If the technology is so mature and safe, why do its operators impose on the rest of us a liability they're unwilling to accept themselves? Why won't the insurance industry—society's expert on risks—insure against this one? And why, ask advocates of free-market principles, should the nuclear industry enjoy a liability cap unavailable to any other industry?

Amary and Hunter Lovins, *Insight*, August 27, 2001.

After shortening the time that nuclear waste remains dangerous to "hundreds of years," the *Houston Chronicle* (4/17/01) declared Yucca Mountain "probably the most studied piece of real estate in the history of the world." It claimed the federal government says the environmental effect of the repository "will be so small as to have essentially no adverse impact on public health and safety," and concluded that "it remains to be seen if there is the political will" to go ahead with the site.

Despite these reassuring claims, Yucca Mountain is in an active seismic area, and growing scientific evidence indicates it is not likely to contain the 70,000 metric tons of spent fuel intended for 10,000 years of undisturbed storage. Scientists from the California Institute of Technology have discovered that the ground around the mountain is expanding at a much faster rate than DOE had originally reported, indicating an increased risk of earthquakes and volcanoes, says Susan Zimmerman, a geologist with the Nevada Agency for Nuclear Projects. Furthermore, the mountain itself has proved to be very leaky; rain water flows through to the aquifer under the mountain in less than 50 years, picking up minerals that lab tests have shown are highly corrosive to the nickel alloy that DOE plans to use for the waste containers.

Nuclear Greenwashing

For more than 10 years, the nuclear industry has been promoting itself as a clean source of energy that, unlike fossil fuels, produces no greenhouse gases or air pollution. Now that global warming has gained more credence in the mainstream press, many media outlets tout this advantage: "Advocates like to claim nuclear power is environmentally friendly because it doesn't contribute to global warming the way fossil fuels do" (NBC, 3/18/01).

Many media outlets pit fossil fuels against nuclear power, as if these choices are our only alternatives. The *Washington Times* (3/18/01) informed its readers that "unlike coal, natural gas and oil-fired power plants, nuclear plants are free not only of carbon emissions but also of other noxious gases like sulfur dioxide, mercury and nitrogen oxide that have made fossil-fuel burning plants the biggest sources of air pollution in the United States."

While nuclear energy does not produce as much CO_2 or other greenhouse gases as, say, coal power, it's inaccurate to call nuclear technology CO_2-free. An enormous amount of electricity is used to enrich the uranium fuel, and the plants that manufacture the fuel in the U.S. are powered by coal plants.

The total impact on the greenhouse effect is not large—comparable to the impact of the processes that create renewable energy, in fact (Renewable Energy Policy Project, 4/00)—but uranium production does have a significant impact on another global environmental threat: ozone depletion. The Environmental Protection Agency's (EPA) Toxic Release Inventory showed that in 1999, the nation's two commercial nuclear fuel-manufacturing plants released 88 percent of the potent, long-lived ozone-depleting chemical CFC-114 by industrial sources in the U.S., and 14 percent of such discharges in the entire world (Louisville *Courier-Journal*, 5/29/01).

As part of their normal operations, nuclear reactors routinely emit radioactive gases and particles into the air. Clusters of cancers, birth defects and various immune disorders have been reported in surrounding communities by citizen groups, but they have not been confirmed because few, if any, resources are allocated to do the necessary studies, says Joe Mangano, national coordinator of the Radiation and Public Health Project.

Selling Safety

The failure of nuclear power in the U.S. is frequently attributed to an irrational public response to the 1979 accident at Three Mile Island, whose only real victim, according to the conventional media narrative, was the nuclear power industry. According to the *Houston Chronicle* (4/17/01), "no one died or was injured because of the release of radioactive material from the plant. More than 2,000 personal injury claims were filed. But after 15 years of litigation, none was upheld." *USA Today* (4/17/01) said the partial meltdown merely "leaked radioactive steam into the atmosphere."

In truth, hundreds of residents living near the plant reported symptoms of radiation poisoning before the accident was even announced. Later, an unusually high number of both strange and common cancers and an array of other health problems started showing up among residents, particularly those living in the path of the radiation plumes that crept over nearby communities during the first few days of the accident. Hundreds of victims have settled lawsuits out of court, but the terms of their settlements remain secret.

After considering the current high price of fossil fuels, mentioning that opponents have safety questions without identifying what they are, and remarking on the high-level waste problem, *NBC Nightly News* (5/3/01) asked if Americans were "over the scare that Three Mile Island created 22 years ago." The answer came from a Georgetown University professor: "There's no way around it, and therefore we have to cope with the consequences." The reporter concluded that "with soaring energy costs, people will soon be more afraid of their utility bills than nuclear power."

A *CBS Evening News* report (5/30/01) on nuclear power in France told viewers that "the giant cooling towers that symbolize some of America's anxiety about atomic power are symbols here of self-assurance." The reporter briefly mentioned concerns about waste and accidents, but ended the story by noting that Paris' nickname, "City of Light," came from "a reputation for progressive thinking."

NBC News' March 19 report ended with the comment that "two decades ago, fear nearly crippled the industry." But then the reporter reassured viewers that "now those fears have receded, and nuclear power could play a huge role in America's energy future."

"[Wind power] has become the fastest growing form of energy production."

The Use of Wind Power Should Be Increased

Birger T. Madsen

In the following viewpoint, Birger T. Madsen argues that wind power could produce at least 20 percent of each continent's energy needs. According to Madsen, improved wind turbines produce more and cheaper electricity than turbines of the past. Unfortunately, he contends, many national governments continue to subsidize conventional energy sources—such as coal and nuclear power—instead of investing in non-polluting, renewable wind power. Birger T. Madsen is managing director of Denmark's BTM Consult Aps, a leading consultancy group specializing in wind power.

As you read, consider the following questions:
1. As cited by Madsen, at what rate is the world's wind energy capacity growing each year?
2. Where are the world's richest wind resources found, according to the author?
3. What steps does the author recommend to increase the world's production of wind energy?

Birger T. Madsen, "Energy's Wind of Change," *UNESCO Courier*, March 2000, p. 9. Copyright © 2000 by *UNESCO Courier*. Reproduced by permission.

It takes a stiff upper lip not to smile when Don Quixote almost falls off his horse in fright after mistaking a windmill for a giant. But perhaps the unlikely hero of Cervantes' literary masterpiece can be credited with foresight. Today's windmills, dubbed wind turbines, dwarf their predecessors, as their steely arms slice through the air at heights of up to 100 metres. More and more of these giants sprout on land and at sea, and they are gaining new ground in the marketplace. And while at present wind power provides just 0.15 per cent of the world's total electricity, it has become the fastest growing form of energy production.

Today's Wind Turbines

The basic principles of wind energy have been known for many centuries. The earliest references to windmills date back to 7th century Persia, but for many the image most closely associated with wind power is that which gave Don Quixote such a fright: a picturesque timber tower supporting four long cloth-covered sails rotating in the wind. Today's wind turbine consists of a giant propeller fixed on top of a tall metal pole. When it rotates, the propeller drives a generator which churns out electricity that can either supply nearby users, possibly in an isolated rural community, or alternatively be sent down a cable hooked up to a central energy grid. One problem is that no way has yet been found of storing electricity to enable the wind's "ups and downs" to be evened out. The trend is for wind farms to move offshore, where their appearance and the sound of whirring propellers won't bother local communities, and strong and steady sea winds will keep the turbines turning at full force.

For the past 25 years, manufacturers have been streamlining components and installing on-board computers to tilt the propeller blades, for example, to suit particular wind conditions. In the early 1980s, the average turbine was 20 metres high with a 26-kilowatt (kW) generator and a rotor diameter of 10.5 metres. A typical turbine today may be perched 55 metres high, have rotors with a diameter of around 50–60 metres and a capacity of up to 1,650 kW. The amount of energy it can produce is equivalent to that consumed by about 350 European households.

Since 1992, more commercial wind farms have been installed in more countries than ever before. There are now 40,000 turbines in 40 countries, and the world's wind energy capacity is growing at nearly 27 per cent annually. In 1998, it topped 10,000 megawatts (MW), about the total energy producing capacity of a country like Denmark. The 1999 figures are not all in, but we know that 1998 was a boom year for the wind power industry. Equipment sales topped $2 billion and there were 35,000 jobs in the sector worldwide. Growth is expected to continue at about 25 per cent a year.

The prime motors of expansion are increasing environmental awareness and political commitments to reduce greenhouse gas emissions made under the Kyoto Protocol of 1997. Wind is free and supplies of it are inexhaustible, and when it produces energy it doesn't release heat or greenhouse gases.

The European Union has taken the lead in rolling out the "green carpets" by introducing tax breaks and investment plans aimed at developing renewable energy sources such as wind power. There are plans to install 40,000 megawatts by the year 2010. Denmark, the wind energy pioneer, covers 10 per cent of its electricity consumption from wind power, delivered from an installed capacity of some 1,700 MW. Germany is quickly catching up, and is now the wind sector's fastest growing market. Spain, with its ample grazing lands and steady winds, is also soon likely to be attracting investment.

Rolling Out a Green Carpet

The climate in the U.S. has been more volatile. Every two years, a congressional battle erupts around the renewal of an important tax credit to spur the industry. The same tumult rattles state legislatures that have their own credit schemes. According to U.S. energy secretary Bill Richardson, wind power should provide five per cent of the nation's electricity demands by the year 2020, compared to the current 0.1 per cent.

For the up and coming energy giants, notably India and China, interest in wind power has less to do with environmental awareness than with economics. These countries where broad swathes of the rural population are without electricity are keen to take advantage of wind investment plans offered by Denmark, Germany and the Netherlands. With nearly 850 MW installed capacity, India ranks first among developing countries and fourth in the world after Germany in the wind power league table. About 600 turbines are churning out 260 MW in China.

Asia and the Pacific used to be considered the coming hot spot for wind power.

However, the region's financial crisis of 1998 knocked many energy investment plans off course, with the notable exception of New Zealand's Tararua Wind Farm—the largest in the southern hemisphere with a capacity of 12 MW.

Faulty Public Perception

In the end, what will make or break wind power is public perception. Earlier in 2002, a citizen's group in Prince Edward County, Ontario, vetoed a modest windfarm project for the coast of Lake Ontario near Hillier. They argued that the 22 proposed wind turbines would be noisy, kill birds and detract from the neighbourhood by being "very visible." These are the most common complaints circulating about windfarms, but at least two of them are weak. From a distance of about 200 metres, the sound of a windfarm is faint. As you approach, the noise is something like the hushed sound of a plane's engines from inside the cabin. Even standing directly under the spinning blades it's possible to carry on a conversation without raising your voice. And as for birds, one Dutch study showed that a small windfarm is far less destructive to bird life than a one-kilometre stretch of road or powerlines.

Really, it's their towering visibility that's got people with lovely lake views worried about windmills on the horizon. Yet the alternative, in these power-parched times, is the construction of more traditional, destructive and decidedly less pretty fossil fuel plants.

Jason Brown, *This Magazine*, July/August 2002.

Turbines are few and far between in South America, aside from a few installations in Costa Rica, Argentina and Brazil. Danish manufacturers are making some inroads into North Africa: Morocco recently installed 50 MW and Egypt 30 MW. The rest of the continent is in the doldrums, an unfortunate state of affairs given the tremendous need for renewable energy, especially in rural areas.

While the world's richest wind resources are found in

North America, China and the former Soviet states, particularly those in Central Asia, we believe that wind power could provide at least 20 per cent of every continent's energy needs. There is enough wind to provide twice the expected global electricity demand for 2020. Even if only 10 per cent of energy needs were met by wind power, the world would be spared about 10 billion tons of carbon emissions (out of a total of 60–70 billion tons). To achieve this goal, 120 times more wind capacity would have to be installed than there is today. The initial investment required would be very high, but operation and maintenance costs would be marginal.

The Costs

Manufacturers today are building bigger and better turbines, and as a result wind-power prices have been falling at about 20 per cent over the past four years. In Denmark, for example, electricity generated by wind power cost almost 17 cents per kilowatt hour (kWh) in the early 1980s. The figure, which covers all costs (equipment, labour, interest on loans, operation and maintenance) fell to 6.15 cents by 1995 and has since dropped to about 4.6 cents. Meanwhile, electricity produced by the installation of a new coal-fired power plant would cost 5 to 6.4 cents kWh, 4 and 5.7 cents kWh in the case of a gas-fired plant, and 4.6 to 6.5 cents kWh in a nuclear facility, according to calculations by UNIPEDE, the European Utility Association.

But while the cost of wind-powered electricity will continue to fall in the future, competitive prices are not enough—there must be a political will to develop the market. Developing countries often find it difficult to raise the capital to cover the steep start-up costs of installing wind turbines. This is the downside of wind power. The initial costs of installing coal-fired plants, for example, are relatively cheap but fuel then has to be imported and in the long run this carbon-based energy will cost more than wind energy. If these countries are to develop an environmentally sound energy sector using wind power, they will need help in finding the initial investment.

The situation is radically different in North America and Western Europe, both of which have enough installed energy capacity to meet demand. In these countries the market for wind energy is driven by environmental considerations rather than economics. If governments do not adopt "green policies" requiring utility companies to close down classical power plants and switch over to renewable energy sources, the market for wind power will not be very dynamic.

Green parties are stepping up the pressure on governments to promote clean energies by helping to fund R&D costs, for example. Other measures that could be taken include subsidizing electricity payments or offering tax credits and low-interest loans for manufacturers. The "polluter pays" principle might also be applied, with a special tax being levied on carbon-emitting energy producers, as opposed to a clean energy source such as wind.

A "Doped" Market

Some argue that a truly promising energy source should not require government support. Others maintain that subsidies will do more harm than good by distorting the energy market and artificially boosting what remains an unpromising alternative. I would argue the contrary—that gas, coal, oil and nuclear energy have been "doped" on state subsidies from the start.

Many power companies using these fuels began as state monopolies protected by national legislation. They control the power grids. Often they bar new energy producers from the grids or impose rules which oblige newcomers to sell their energy at unfair prices. The development of wind power has also been hurt by the absence of legislation. For example, the UK has the best wind resources in Europe, but commercial attempts to set up wind farms in the last three years were stymied when local authorities failed to issue permits for turbine construction. Had the national government set up guidelines and policies inciting local authorities to cooperate, there might be more wind farms in Britain today.

The two notable champions of wind power are Denmark and Germany. Ferociously anti-nuclear, the public in both these countries studied their energy options before giving wind a "green light". Their diligence is now paying off at home and abroad, as their turbines blow a fresh breeze into global energy production.

| *"By moving to the hydrogen economy, we will return to making our living within the steady income energies of nature."*

Hydrogen Will Be the Energy Source of the Future

Ty Cashman and Bret Logue

In the following viewpoint, Ty Cashman and Bret Logue contend that hydrogen will eventually replace fossil fuels as the world's main energy source. Such a change will be beneficial, they argue, because unlike fossil fuels, hydrogen is renewable and nonpolluting when burned. Cashman and Logue explain that hydrogen—which can be made from wind- and solar-generated electricity—can be burned like natural gas to power home heating systems, certain modes of transportation, and manufacturing plants. Ty Cashman is president of the Solar Economy Institute, and Bret Logue is a policy analyst and entreprenuer.

As you read, consider the following questions:

1. When hydrogen is burned, what is its only emission, as reported by Cashman and Logue?
2. Why do the authors think that fuel cells will not initiate the hydrogen economy despite predictions that they will?
3. As cited by the authors, how much would it cost to convert an individual gasoline-powered car to use hydrogen fuel?

Ty Cashman and Bret Logue, "The Coming Hydrogen Economy," *Yes! A Journal of Positive Futures*, Fall 2001, pp. 40–42. Copyright © 2001 by Ty Cashman and Bret Logue. Reproduced by permission.

The day is crystal blue as you pull into a refueling station in your sleek silver SUV. Despite being an advocate for a green Earth, the demands of your life—three kids, a German shepherd, and a work-at-home husband—were greater than your compact car could handle. So a year ago, in 2009, you made your first payment on a brand new vehicle. It has a tremendous amount of cargo space, a comfy interior, and—surprisingly—no steering wheel. Instead, a cockpit-style stick gives you precision control as you maneuver up to the pump. But what is most shocking of all is that the $1.50-per-pound fuel that powers your car is not gasoline, but the emission-free fuel that has been all the rage since its introduction in 2004: hydrogen.

Progress at the Pump

You pop open the fuel cap and slide the nozzle end of the hose securely onto a shiny silver receptacle. A "ding" from the pump reassures you that the seal is tight and you turn to watch the fuel meter as hydrogen quickly fills the compressed gas tank located in the back of the car. When the car is running, the hydrogen powers a fuel cell that generates electricity via a low-temperature chemical reaction. In the fuel cell, hydrogen combines with oxygen, producing electricity to power electric motors that move the car and emit only water vapor as exhaust. Additional efficiency is gained by recovering energy produced during braking and storing it for the next acceleration.

Half of the car's hydrogen tank was filled yesterday by solar cells covering the roof of your home. As the noonday sun baked the solar cells, a small electrolyzer separated the H_2O from a container of filtered waste-water into hydrogen and oxygen and stored the hydrogen until you returned home. Then, the car's tank was filled partway with this homemade hydrogen. The trip to the pump today was for the five pounds of additional hydrogen needed for a full tank. This hydrogen comes from a wind farm in a mountain pass that you can see in the distance. As you slide your credit card to pay your $7.50 fuel bill, you gloat a little, knowing that you'll not need to refill the tank of your fuel cell-powered SUV Hypercar for another 500 miles.

The Need for Hydrogen

In 2001, we are in the endgame of the Fossil Economy. Nobody doubts this. The only question is whether the end will come sooner or later. Energy analysts know what comes next: the Solar Hydrogen Economy. The US Department of Energy confirms that hydrogen technologies "will provide America with near-, mid-, and long-term strategies for a clean, sustainable, domestic energy supply." The Fossil Economy is coming to an end because the supply of petroleum is dwindling—with less oil discovered every day than is being burned. But much more seriously, the release of additional fossil carbon into the Earth's atmospheric carbon cycle has the potential of tipping that cycle into an accelerated feedback loop of self-reinforced heating, called a "runaway" greenhouse effect.

According to the United Nations Intergovernmental Panel on Climate Change, the world needs to reduce greenhouse gas emissions by 60–70 percent to effectively prevent increased global warming. A reduction as dramatic as that entails abandoning fossil fuels as the central energy source for the world's societies. Switching to renewable hydrogen can do the trick—without radical economic dislocations. The Solar Hydrogen Economy is inevitable. The only issue is whether we can bring it about quickly, or whether the transition will be stalled by vested interests until it is too late to prevent the runaway greenhouse effect.

The Solar Hydrogen Economy

What is a Solar Hydrogen Economy? It is any economy (it could be either high tech or low tech) in which the fuel for cooking, home heating, transportation, electricity, and production of goods and services comes directly or indirectly from the sun, the wind, renewable biomass, or ocean energies. All of these energy sources derive from the sun. All can generate electricity to convert water to hydrogen. Either electricity or hydrogen fuel can be used for nearly any energy application.

Hydrogen can be made from wind-generated and solar-generated electricity by electrolysis, a process of running electricity through water that separates the H_2O molecules into hydrogen and oxygen gases. Only two gallons of water are necessary to make one gallon of gasoline equivalent hydrogen.

Hydrogen burns like natural gas, but it is completely clean. When it burns it releases only water vapor. It is as safe or safer than any common fuel in use today. It can fuel your cook stove, warm your house, power internal combustion cars, as well as buses, trains, and aircraft. In addition, it is the most direct source of fuel for fuel cells, which are highly efficient electric power plants that can be used to power cars or to provide electricity and heat in buildings.

Producing Affordable Hydrogen

Today's state-of-the-art wind turbines are producing electricity for 4 cents a kilowatt hour before any subsidies. (For comparison, the average wholesale electricity price in California eighteen months ago was three cents; a year ago 10 cents; six months ago 31 cents.) Wind power is immune to erratic fuel prices and is fully competitive today with electricity from fossil fuels.

Electrolyzed hydrogen from wind power would cost somewhat more than its per-energy equivalent in gasoline sold at the pump today, but hydrogen's greater efficiency in vehicles would help narrow the difference on a per-mile basis. For example, if in an adapted combustion engine, hydrogen could provide 50 percent more mileage per equivalent unit of energy than gasoline provides, then, even if hydrogen were to cost twice as much as gasoline, the cost-per-mile for hydrogen would be only a little more than gasoline. Fuel cells are expected to be more than twice as efficient as current gasoline engines, which means that even if hydrogen costs twice as much at the pump, the per mile cost for hydrogen will be less than for gasoline.

During the start-up period, we can expect some portion of hydrogen to come from natural gas (CH_4). To prevent the release of CO_2 in the steam created by hydrogen production, Robert Williams of Princeton has suggested that the CO_2 be pumped back down the gas well to re-pressurize it and extend its useful life. The capture and disposal of CO_2 adds 25–30 percent to the cost of hydrogen produced by the steam reforming of natural gas. A new process called thermocatalytic decomposition is being developed that would produce hydrogen from natural gas without carbon dioxide emissions, thus not require sequestration. Carbon is extracted during the process as carbon black, a valuable material that could be sold for $100 or more per ton.

Wiley. © 1991 by *San Francisco Examiner*. Reprinted with permission.

Eventually, with high demand and mass production, electricity from solar thermal electric power plants and photovoltaic cells will become competitive with gasoline.

Making the Transition

Originally, it was thought that fuel cells would initiate the hydrogen economy. They are efficient, clean and have no moving parts. But they are still in the development stage and the costs are still high. At present the cost of fuel cells is hovering at $1,500–$2,000/kW, more than 10 times what would be a competitive cost for transportation. Although most people in the industry expect the price to come down as the volume of units purchased increases, it is unclear how long it will take before fuel cells become competitive for the transportation market. It could be 8–10 years.

Fortunately, initiating the hydrogen economy may not depend entirely on cheap fuel cells. There are other uses of hydrogen that can serve as a bridge to fuel cells over the next 5–10 years. Larger hybrid cars with internal combustion engines are expected soon. If their engines are adapted to use hydrogen, the combined efficiencies will be high and the cost per mile of hydrogen reasonable.

In addition, there are no overwhelming technological barriers to converting most of the 200 million vehicles on the highways in America today (and the 800 million worldwide) to use hydrogen fuel. Engineers estimate a company that converted 100,000 cars a year could convert an individual car to hydrogen fuel for less than $2,500. Although there are no conversion kits available today, a well-coordinated local or regional political initiative might initiate this process.

The construction of the first hydrogen refueling stations strategically placed in regional corridors could begin at the same time as the introduction of these hydrogen vehicles. Neither would have to *come first*. This would solve the so-called "chicken and egg problem."

Municipal buses and city government vehicle fleets can also be hydrogen fueled without waiting for a refueling infrastructure, since they return to the same fueling station at night. Local and regional initiatives will be what provide us with a smooth and steady pathway to the hydrogen economy.

While hydrogen will be somewhat more expensive than gasoline in the early years of its introduction, this could easily be offset by collecting a portion of its extra cost from the price of gasoline. This mechanism is termed a "feebate": the cost of hydrogen and gasoline at the pump are kept the same by collecting the extra cost of hydrogen from a slightly increased gasoline price. Because the cost of the feebate on the relatively small volumes of hydrogen fuel would be spread over the infinitely larger volumes of gasoline, the impact of the feebate would not become noticeable to the consumer until hydrogen comprised roughly 10 percent of the total market. By then, the costs of producing hydrogen are likely to have dropped substantially.

Because hydrogen is the least dense substance in the universe, it must be compressed significantly to be able to supply energy equivalent to a comparable volume of gasoline. Compression tanks have been designed and crash-tested to address this issue. An average internal combustion engine in today's cars gets only 27 miles to a gallon of gasoline. A tank of hydrogen, compressed at 5,000 psi, would give the car a range of 190 miles. This tank will be larger, but lighter, than a tank of gasoline. Hydrogen is three times lighter than gasoline per Btu. (Tanks that carry compressed gases for industrial purposes are commonly at 3,500 psi. Pressures between 4,000 and 5,000 psi will soon be common.) According to the Electric Power Research Institute, 40 percent of all personal cars in the US are driven no more than 20 miles a day, and many millions more are driven less than 40 miles a day. Thus, a moderate-sized, 5,000 psi compressed hydrogen tank would get the range necessary to make many hydrogen vehicles viable.

Local Politics Can Do It

The conversion to a hydrogen economy is not a problem of limited technologies but of political priorities. Citizens can influence the leadership at the state and regional levels even without federal cooperation. Visionary mayors can create the first "Hydrogen Cities." Local citizens can join in regional task forces for finding the green energy sources appropriate for their geographic area. Cities can join with neighboring municipalities to create Regional Hydrogen Utility Districts, planning and implementing hydrogen refueling corridors, converting municipal fleets or bus services to run on hydrogen, and accessing potential sites for the introduction of stationary fuel cells, such as schools, police headquarters, or local airports.

Years ago, [American architect and inventor] Buckminster Fuller saw fossil fuels as the "starter motor" for the industrial-technological society. He said it is time to move from the starter motor to the main engines, which are solar, wind, and ocean energies. By moving to the hydrogen economy, we will return to making our living within the steady income energies of nature. If we can shift from the starter motor to the main engines in time to prevent global warming, we may yet acquire the wisdom to direct the rest of our technologies towards a more positive effect on the living world.

"*Wave energy has been hailed as the most promising renewable source for maritime countries.*"

Wave Energy Is a Promising Energy Source

David Ross

According to David Ross in the following viewpoint, the energy from ocean waves will soon be producing large amounts of electricity for maritime countries. He explains that despite the potential of the sea to destroy wave-energy stations, several nations have made progress in designing indestructible small-scale stations. These stations use waves to run a turbine, which produces electricity. David Ross is author of several books on wave energy, including *Energy from the Waves*, *Power from the Waves*, and *Scuppering the Waves*.

As you read, consider the following questions:

1. According to Ross, when did the interest in harnessing wave energy first emerge?
2. What is an oscillating water column, as defined by the author?
3. In Ross's opinion, what is the biggest obstacle to harnessing wave energy?

David Ross, "Give Us a Wave!" *Our Planet*, vol. 12, 2002, pp. 30–31. Copyright © 2002 by *Our Planet*. Reproduced by permission.

W ave energy has been hailed as the most promising renewable source for maritime countries. It does no environmental damage and is inexhaustible—the waves go on for ever. It is invariably popular with the public, which has a sentimental love of the sea.

Great Potential

The potential resource is vast. It is usually estimated as being of the order of 2,000 gigawatts (GW), though UNESCO [United Nations Educational, Scientific, and Cultural Organization] has put it at roughly double that amount. But what we need to estimate is how much can be gathered and delivered at an economic price. Getting energy from the waves has been studied since the time of the French Revolution when the first patent was filed in Paris by a father and son named Girard. They noted that 'the enormous mass of a ship of the line, which no other known force is capable of lifting, responds to the slightest wave motions'.

There was little progress in turning those motions into useful energy until the last quarter century, mainly through lack of scientific knowledge of what a wave was, how it travelled and how it could be converted. There was also a well-deserved respect for the formidable nature of the task, and the considerable capital needed was not available.

Unlike hydro-electric power it cannot draw on the flow of water running in one direction. You cannot put a water wheel in the sea and leave it to revolve and generate electricity, even though, to the watcher on the shore, it appears that the waves are advancing towards the beach in a straight line. Leonardo da Vinci noted that when the wind blew across a field of corn, it looked as though waves of corn ran across the field—whereas, in fact, the individual heads were only moving slightly. So it is with waves in the sea, which can also be compared with the movement of a skipping rope. As one end is waggled, a wave form travels to the other—but the rope itself does not advance.

Elusive Power

A wave travels forward in an elusive, up-and-down motion. Its height is the key indication of its power. So the rougher the sea, the more potentially fruitful it is—but also the harder it is to harvest. So wave energy engineers have to design a power station that can absorb the power of the most ferocious waves without being wrecked. Two, in Scotland and Norway, have already been victims of the sea.

Yoshio Masuda, from Japan, invented the oscillating water column (OWC)—effectively a chimney which stands on the seabed and admits the waves through an opening near to its base. As they rise and fall in the open sea outside, the height of the column of water inside rises and falls too. As the water level rises, air is forced up and out through a turbine which spins and drives the generator. As it falls again, air is sucked back in from the atmosphere to fill the resulting vacuum and once again the turbo-generator is activated.

Creative Technology

One of [the ways we can harness the sea's energy] would be to use the difference between sea levels. In Egypt, water running through an underground canal linking the Mediterranean to the El-Qattara depression could be used to generate electricity. In Israel, the same principle could be used in a canal between the Mediterranean and the Dead Sea which would gradually descend 400 metres.

France Bequette, *UNESCO Courier*, July/August 1998.

Professor Alan Wells of Queen's University, Belfast, greatly improved the efficiency of the invention by devising a turbine which spins in the same direction regardless of whether the air is being pushed out or sucked back into the chimney.

Norway launched a wave energy station on the coast close to Bergen in 1985, which combines an OWC standing facing the waves, with a Norwegian invention called a Tapchan (from the words tapered channel). The waves ride up a concrete slope to a point 3 metres above sea level, where they splash into a reservoir. The water flows back to the ocean through a turbine which drives a generator.

Professor Stephen Salter of Edinburgh University has contributed the most intellectual invention. Salter's Duck, as it is called, looks charming and popularized the idea of wave power. It is also a potential world-beater. The ducks are cones, filled with sophisticated electronic equipment, built around a spine, which bob up and down on the waves driving a generator. Salter will not let the system go to sea until he feels it is ready.

Wave Energy on a Small Scale

Small-scale wave power initiatives—from 100 kilowatts (kW) to 2 megawatts (MW)—are now going ahead in more than a dozen countries. Scotland had an experimental 75kW OWC on the shore of the island of Islay for 11 years: this has now been replaced by a 500kW model, named the Limpet, clinging to rocks facing waves sweeping in from 5,000 kilometres of the Atlantic.

The same group of researchers plans a 2MW seagoing device called the Osprey. Another Scottish model, called Pelamis, is a series of cylinders linked by hinged joints and hydraulic motors driving generators.

Portugal has been working for several years on an OWC on the island of Pico in the Azores. The Netherlands has invented the Archimedes Wave Swing, an air-filled 'floater' which moves up and down while its 'ground floor' sits on the seabed. An American company is working on a 10MW scheme based on buoys 3 kilometres off the south coast of Australia. India, China, Sweden and Japan are among other countries where wave energy is burgeoning.

Overcoming Hurdles

The technical problems have been steadily overcome but the only practical applications have been on a small scale. Wave energy is crying out for 2,000MW power stations in the deep ocean.

The big hurdle is financial. Wave energy was not devised to save money but to save the world. Early researchers used to say optimistically that the energy was free because the gods provided the waves. Others swung to the opposite extreme by using high discount rates, which hit wave energy unfairly because it is a capital-intensive technology, where most of the expenditure is during construction. The simple way to change the costing is to change the discount rate.

The energy establishment has not been helpful; it naturally did not welcome a new rival for its markets. Governments and companies emphasized conventional costing. A leading Netherlands inventor commented: 'The financial engineering is even more difficult than the technical engineering. In our team, we call it emotional engineering'. But, for the first time for 30 years, the breakthrough is now in sight. Wave electricity will be on the grid in many countries before long.

Periodical Bibliography

The following articles have been selected to supplement the diverse views presented in this chapter.

Jason Brown	"Winds of Change," *This Magazine*, July/August 2002.
CQ Researcher	"Energy and the Environment," March 3, 2000.
CQ Researcher	"Renewable Energy," November 7, 1997.
Mark C. Fitzgerald	"Renewable Energy Today and Tomorrow," *World & I*, March 1999.
Patrice Hill	"Energy Crisis Rekindles Interest in Nuclear Power," *Insight*, April 23, 2001.
Ray W. Kosanke	"Why Not Solar Now?" *Electronic News*, January 29, 2001.
James A. Lake	"Can Nuclear Power Solve the Energy Crisis? Yes: Nuclear-Power Generation Is Cost-Efficient, Reliable, Safe and Emits No Air Pollutants," *Insight*, August 27, 2001.
Marianne Lavelle, Harvey Black, and Cynthia Salter	"Wind-Power Revolution," *U.S. News & World Report*, November 12, 2001.
Roy McAlister	"Tapping Energy from Solar Hydrogen," *World & I*, February 1999.
Joachim Milberg	"Make Way for the Zero-Litre Car," *Our Planet*, March 2002.
Marilyn L. Nemzer, Anna K. Carter, and Kenneth P. Nemzer	"Geothermal Energy Facts," December 23, 2000, http://geothermal.org.
Charles Platt	"Cold Fusion Is Real?" *Wired*, November 1998.
Matt Scanlon	"Not Your Mother's Solar Power Anymore," *Mother Earth News*, January 2001.
William Underhill	"Taking the Breeze: Electricity," *Newsweek*, April 15, 2002.
Jack Wakeland	"Environmentalism's Big Lie: Renewable Energy," *Intellectual Activist*, August 2001.

CHAPTER 4

How Can Global Resources Be Protected?

Chapter Preface

Tourists watch endangered cheetahs on safaris in Kenya and witness rare birds in the canopy of the Amazon rain forest. They research the habits of blue whales in Mexico, test water samples in the Bahamas, and sail through the air on swings in Costa Rican forests. People engaged in these activities are participating in the fastest-growing sector of the tourism industry—ecotourism.

The Ecotourism Society defines ecotourism as "responsible travel to natural areas, which conserves the environment and sustains the wellbeing of the local people." Recognizing the adverse impact of resource-extracting operations such as oil drilling and logging, many developing nations are opting instead to open their sensitive lands to ecotourists. Ecotourism can enable local people to earn money without degrading the environment and provides conservative-minded Westerners the opportunity to see and protect fragile ecosystems. Indeed, ecotourism has become so popular that it is now a $425 billion industry. However, despite the highly touted benefits of ecotourism, it has been the center of heated controversy since its inception.

Those who support ecotourism claim that it helps local people in developing nations move toward a more sustainable method of development. Conservation International explains that "attempting to provide for their families, local people have cleared rain forests to grow crops, raise cattle, or harvest timber. This predicament creates a pressing need to provide locals with alternative income sources which will deter deforestation and other habitat loss." Ralf Buckley, a professor of ecotourism at Griffith University in Australia, argues that "if tourism can help protect relatively undisturbed areas from those higher-impact uses, then it can contribute to conservation even though it has some negative impact itself." Advocates applaud operations such as one in Belize that has moved local fishermen out of the destructive gill-net-fishing industry into tourist-oriented catch-and-release fly-fishing outfits. Andy Drumm, director of Nature Conservancy's International Conservation Program, reports that the Belize fishermen are "making four times as much in a year as they were before."

However, critics of ecotourism contend that there are far fewer success stories than supporters claim. Deborah McLaren, director of Rethinking Ecotourism, argues that developers indiscriminately slap the ecotourism label on any project, no matter how destructive the operation. To illustrate, she describes a magazine article she read about an ecotourism operation in Costa Rica: "When I opened the article, to read it, it was about someone building a huge resort with golf courses displacing local communities. It was greenwashing." Megan Epler Wood of the Ecotourism Society reports that timber around Nepal's Himalayan trails has been stripped to heat water for trekkers, and nature guide Ruth Norris claims that cheetah ecosafaris traumatize the big cats. As Linda Baker explains in *Lingua Franca*, critics think of ecotourism as "a veritable Trojan horse of globalization, a misguided development project foisted on unwilling—and unsuspecting—Third World communities." Those opposed to ecotourism contend that it is counterproductive because it actually encourages development in nations' most ecologically sensitive regions.

The United Nations General Assembly designated 2002 the "International Year of Ecotourism." But critics want the name changed to the "International Year of *Reviewing* Ecotourism." The idea of going on safari in Kenya or trekking through the Amazon rain forest certainly appeals to environmentally conscious Westerners who believe that their tourist dollars will help preserve global resources, but the verdict is still out about whether such optimism is justified. In the following chapter, authors debate other ways to protect the world's resources. As the debate over ecotourism illustrates, maximizing human welfare while limiting humanity's adverse impact on the environment remains a perennial challenge.

"Population stabilization efforts can no longer be ignored as unnecessary preparations or unwarranted panic mongering."

Stabilizing the World's Population Growth Will Protect Global Resources

Werner Fornos

According to Werner Fornos in the following viewpoint, the fears of nineteenth-century reverend Thomas Malthus concerning human population growth may prove true. As Malthus predicted, population growth is outpacing humans' capacity to feed themselves, Fornos contends, and is leading to environmental degradation. Moreover, Fornos argues that technological advancements cannot postpone a global catastrophe indefinately. He urges societies to adopt population stabilization policies before natural checks, such as famine and disease, lead to the deaths of millions. Werner Fornos is president of the Population Institute, a Washington-based nonprofit public interest group, and a frequent speaker and writer on population issues.

As you read, consider the following questions:
1. What is the core of Malthus's theory, as stated by Fornos?
2. According to the author, how many people are added to the world's population every year?
3. Why does Fornos think that the loss of plant species such as the yew is a serious problem?

Werner Fornos, "Back to Malthus: 200-Year-Old Scenario May Return to Haunt Us," *The Social Contract*, Spring 1998, pp. 188–95. Copyright © 1998 by The Social Contract Press. Reproduced by permission.

M ost prophets have been consigned to the trash bin at some point in human history, only to be retrieved, resurrected, and sometimes even beatified. Prophets and visionaries, by definition, cannot be judged during their lifetimes. In the fields of economics and other social sciences, no one has been more discredited than the Reverend Thomas Robert Malthus, who has been more recognized in derision than in serious contemplation.

Revisiting Malthus

As the world continues to grow exponentially as the English parson had warned us, the relevance of his thinking becomes as clear as the summer sky. Two hundred years after he first wrote his "anonymous" *Essay on the Principle of Population*, few miracles, it appears, can save the world from careless growth. A careful study of the Rev. Malthus' theories, principles, likely outcomes and possible solutions makes one thing clear: for all their mistiming and misconceptions, Malthus' fears are at our world's threshold again. Now, more than at any other time in history, we must heed his warnings, notwithstanding the dismissive claims of the so-called optimists.

Credible and incontrovertible evidence is presented almost every day that points to a growing imbalance between population growth and the world's resources. There is still hope, and possible room, for yet another technological miracle, but any such breakthrough cannot wipe out fears of a food crisis forever: it can only postpone it for a little longer. There is a limit to available croplands in the world, and statistics indicate a gradual fall in per capita cropland use and food grain output already.

We can no longer rest on our hope for technology to carry us through another crisis. Alongside a search for more efficient ways to feed our billions we also must work to reduce the number of mouths to feed, as Malthus himself recommended. Population stabilization efforts can no longer be ignored as unnecessary preparations or unwarranted panic mongering. A reassessment of Malthus will give us that most essential inspiration to make the world more livable. . . .

What makes the Malthusian theory harsh are both the sweeping conclusion and the rather bleak scenario it projects for the late 18th and the early 19th century England—so much so that the word Malthusian has become synonymous with "pessimistic."

The core of his theory was that population grows in geometrical proportions—multiplying at the rates of 1, 2, 4, 8, 16, etc., and doubling every 25 years—while food production can grow only in arithmetic progressions—1, 2, 3, 4, 5, etc.—and therefore at some point in the future ("in a thousand years") population growth will overwhelm food production. When such a time arrives, the theory concludes, misery and vice will act as checks on population growth, and again bring about a balance between the two.

Malthus based his theory on two postulata, assumptions that are as valid today as they were 200 years ago:

> First, that food is necessary for the existence of man. Secondly, that the passion between the sexes is necessary and will remain nearly in its present state.

The weight of the Utopians' criticism was directed at his conjectured rates of growth of population (geometrical) and food production (arithmetical). Malthus extrapolated his theory from real-life experiences of the time, and in 18th century England his projections for food production seemed even generous. He had no way of foreseeing that science would revolutionize agriculture with steam engine, biochemistry and plant genetics.

So, mechanization and the green revolution boosted global food production, especially in the 20th century, and fortunately the world did not see the kind of widespread famine and starvation Malthus expected. Falling fertility in Europe, in fact, threatened to prove contrary to Malthusian projections—the problem of underpopulation. But the specter of the "Malthusian trap" was never completely removed. . . .

The Malthusian Trap

Today, more than ever in the past, the Malthusian trap is staring us straight in the face. Malthus reached his famous ratio on population growth and food production on the basis of the newly independent colonies of North America, where population was doubling every 25 years, but food production was only adding one more proportion over the base year. The world's population today will not double in 25 years—because as the population base grows larger it will take longer for the population to double—but the growth rate is as alarming as Malthus feared.

It took the world population a hundred years to move from 1 billion in 1830 to 2 billion in 1930, but only 30 years to reach the third billion in 1960; 15 years to reach the fourth billion in 1975, and 12 years to reach 5 billion in 1987. It is expected to reach 6 billion sometime in 1999. Thus, even at this huge size, world population is set to double in less than 40 years—from 3 billion in 1960 to 6 billion in 1999.

There are at least 74 countries, 40 of them in Africa, whose populations are doubling within 30 years or less. Not coincidentally, these countries also happen to be the ones struggling the most to feed their millions. Every year more than 80 million people are added to the world's population. About 98 percent of the annual increase occurs in poor developing countries in Asia and Africa whose capacity to meet the basic needs of their peoples is far from adequate.

As I pointed out in my recent testimony before the Foreign Operations Subcommittee of the U.S. House of Representatives Committee on Appropriations, the enormous momentum in population growth set off by the entry of nearly 3 billion people—a number equal to the entire population of the world as recently as 1960—into their reproductive years in the next generation will have the largest impact on future population growth.

Population in the Developing World

Eighty percent of the world lives in less developed countries. The share of the more developed world is expected to fall from the present 20 percent to 16 percent in 2020. Europe and, to a lesser extent, North America, may have turned into Adam Smith's "pampered fine lady" and slowed down population growth in economic prosperity, but Africa has become a shocking laboratory to prove the Malthusian theory.

The continent, now home to 750 million people, has been growing at the staggering annual rate of 2.6 percent. Most African countries have total fertility rates of six children or more per woman. True to the other end of the Malthusian equation, Africa is also the least self-sufficient in food production. The continent is largely covered with deserts and has little arable land. Most African countries, beaten at the marketplace, look up to food aid from rich Western countries.

Misery and pestilence, the main Malthusian checks to population growth, are also in evidence in Africa where millions are killed in wars, carnage, and in famines caused by floods and drought. Thousands of African lives are also claimed every year by diseases such as AIDS, the worst pestilence of the modern age, and by Ebola virus and Dengue fever.

Feeding the Millions

Driven to Utopian optimism by the phenomenal success of science in multiplying global food production, critics have been quick to trash Malthusian predictions as shortsighted scare mongering. Ignorant as he was of the scientific miracle in store for the world, Malthus allowed room for such a scenario in his limited assessment:

> No limits whatever are placed to the productions of the earth; they may increase for ever and be greater than any assignable quantity; yet still the power of population being a power of a superior order, the increase of the human species can only be kept commensurate to the increase of the means of subsistence by the constant operation of the strong law of necessity acting as a check upon the greater power.

So far, the world's food production has managed to keep pace with population growth and may do so for some years to come. There are signs everywhere, however, that the "fruits of the earth" cannot be taken to be infinite. We of the 20th–21st centuries have already seen the near-saturation of the technological miracle that helped boost food production. While another technological revolution to improve the world's resource reserves may not yet be ruled out, to place all hopes in that invisible cornucopia would be foolhardy.

The Green Revolution of the 1960s and 1970s, driven by the development of better varieties of food grains and more efficient use of croplands, gave rise to euphoric complacency. However, according to agricultural scientists and policy experts, the growth has apparently hit a plateau. Lester R. Brown of the Worldwatch Institute warns us that 200 years after Malthus wrote his *Essay*, "the race between food and people is still a matter of concern in many national capitals."

From 1950 to 1990, the world's grain farmers raised the productivity of their land by an unprecedented 2.1 percent a year, but since 1990 the rise has slowed markedly. Rice production, which grew at the rate of 2.1 percent annually between 1960 and 1990, has dropped to 1 percent since 1990; wheat yields dropped from 2.6 percent annual growth to 1 percent, and corn productivity fell from 2.6 percent to 1.7 percent. During the same period, world population has been growing at the annual rate of 1.5 percent. Could it be that the Malthusian specter is revisiting us, revalidating fears of population growth over-whelming food production?

"The slower rise in world grainland productivity during the 1990s may mark the transition from a half-century dominated by food surpluses to a future that will be dominated by food scarcity," Brown warns.

A 70-day supply of grain in carryover stocks is considered desirable for a minimum level of food security. However, since 1996, it has been hovering around a 50- to 55-day supply.

Environmental Degradation

Even as the world's farmers race to feed the billions, large stretches of farmland are lost to soil erosion, salinization and other forms of degradation. The Global Land Assessment of Soil Degradation (Glasod) estimates that of the nearly 8 billion acres which are under pasture, 21 percent are degraded, while of the 3.7 billion acres in cropland, 38 percent are degraded to various degrees. The degradation of cropland is most extensive in Africa, affecting 65 percent of the cropland area, compared with 51 percent in Latin America and 38 percent in Asia.

Farming in most of the developed world depends heavily on irrigation, but water has become one of the scarcest commodities of the modern world. According to recent reports, 1.5 billion people—nearly one-quarter of the world population—lack an adequate supply of drinking water. As many as 39 countries are expected to suffer severe water deficiency by 2050. Not surprisingly, 35 of these countries are set to double their populations by that year.

The growing urbanization of the world also results in the diversion of agricultural land into such uses as housing, industrial and recreational sites. The World Resources Institute estimates that since World War II, nearly 3 billion acres—equivalent to the combined area of China and India—have been impaired as a consequence of human activity.

Toles. © 1990 by *The Buffalo News*. Reprinted by permission of Universal Press Syndicate.

With the shrinking of farmland, people resort to extreme, environmentally dangerous steps to sustain farming. Thousands of square miles of forests have been burnt in desperate attempts to gain croplands in several parts of the world. More than 19,000 square miles of Amazon rain forests have been burning for over two months in 1998, destroying several animal and plant species. Fires set off by firewood-seekers in Indonesia earlier in 1998 caused severe air pollution throughout Southeast Asia. According to estimates, year after year the world is losing some 28 million acres of forest, more than two-thirds of which is converted to unsustainable agricultural purposes.

"Half of the forests that once covered the earth are gone, and deforestation has been accelerating in the last 30 years," says a recent Worldwatch report. "Each year, at least another 39 million acres of natural forest are razed—an area the size of Washington State," the report says.

Conflicts with Nature and Other Species

As the demand for food presses against the available cropland, humankind's dogged effort to extend its turf invariably comes into conflicts with Nature and other species. Pushed to the limits of croplands, the human species turns to the world's oceans to supplement nourishment. As giant trawlers scrape the ocean floor to increase fish output, the marine ecosystem is gradually and irredeemably destroyed. Most of the world's fish species are either over-exploited or exploited near their replacement levels.

According to the World Conservation Union's first comprehensive Red List, published recently, 12.5 percent of the world's 270,000 known species of plants are found at risk of extinction. In the United States, 29 percent of the 16,108 plant species are on the imperiled list. Many of these plants are essential in producing life-saving drugs. For example, 75 percent of the yew family, which produces the anti-cancer drug taxol, is threatened with extinction, according to the Union.

As the world struggles to feed, clothe and shelter the growing millions, the delicate balance among animals, plants, natural resources and the atmosphere is severely disturbed. A now-familiar strain of the call for sustainable development in consonance with the earth's carrying capacity can be read in Malthus's revised *Essay*, where he suggests efforts to balance population with "provisions" of sustenance.

Checks to Population Growth—Malthusian and Modern

Explaining the delicate balance between population and resources and its consequences Malthus wrote:

> Through the animal and vegetable kingdoms, nature has scattered the seeds of life abroad with the most profuse and liberal hand. She has been comparatively sparing in the room and the nourishment necessary to rear them. The germs of

existence contained in this spot of earth, with ample food and ample room to expand in, would fill millions of worlds in the course of a few thousand years. Necessity, that imperious all pervading law of nature, restrains them within the prescribed bounds. The race of plants and the race of animals shrink under this great restrictive law. And the race of man cannot, by any efforts of reason, escape from it. Among plants and animals its effects are waste of seed, sickness and premature death. Among mankind, misery and vice. The former, misery, is an absolutely necessary consequence of it. Vice is a highly probable consequence, and we therefore see it abundantly prevail, but it ought not, perhaps, to be called an absolutely necessary consequence.

Malthus suggests an oscillatory effect between population growth and the welfare level of society: population grows beyond sustenance; famine, diseases and high mortality, especially among children, ensue, thus reducing population growth, even as surviving members of society toil harder to produce more food to meet the demand. The suggestion that disease and starvation will check population explosion may sound out-of tune with the medical advancements of this age, but starvation and diseases continue to haunt millions of people all over the world.

More than 20 million adults worldwide are infected with AIDS, which has led to an increase in mortality in Africa—to more than one-and-a-half times the world average—and brought down life expectancy to 50 years or less in several African countries. Infant and maternal mortality rates continue to be high in several parts of the world.

Recent reports have also indicated a return of infectious and parasitic diseases such as malaria, tuberculosis, cholera, dengue fever and Ebola. More than 17 million people have died from these diseases since 1995, accounting for more than one-fourth of all deaths. About 97 percent of these deaths occur in low-income countries that also have high fertility rates.

On a more humane level, Malthus also prescribes other checks on population which are within the control of the people—the very ideas promoted by the modern-day demographers and sociologists:

> . . . a foresight of the difficulties attending the hearing of family acts as a preventive check and the actual distresses of

some of the lower classes, by which they are disabled from giving proper food and attention to their children, acts as a positive check to the natural increase of population.

In the revised edition of the *Essay*, Malthus was less pessimistic about the future happiness of society and added one more possible check to population: delayed marriage, which he termed "moral restraint."

It is clearly the duty of each individual not to marry till he has a prospect of supporting his children; but it is at the same time to be wished that he should retain undiminished his desire of marriage, in order that he may exert himself to realize this prospect, and be stimulated to make provision for the support of greater numbers.

Of course, modern contraception was inconceivable in Malthus's time; nor could one expect the parson to recommend abortion. So within the constraints of the time the best solution he could find was delayed marriage and childbearing, which continue to be among the prime strategies of population stabilization advocates today. Several international studies have revealed that delayed marriage has helped many countries slow down their population growths. . . .

More Is Not Merrier

Malthus's detractors, bent on proving his theory wrong, claim that the earth's resources, even at present levels, can sustain 11 billion or 15 billion people—more than double the current population. They claim that the recoverable stocks of various metals and minerals in the earth can sustain us for thousands of years to come. But the signs of the times show more strain on the resources than comfort.

Emboldened by Paul Ehrlich's failed wager with the late Julian Simon on metal prices in the 1980s, the cornucopians say science, that ultimate provider of hope, can devise technologies to recover mineral wealth from the core of the earth. An improved method of fast extraction and exploitation of natural resources (oil and other minerals) may increase the current output levels, but it does not mean the resources are infinite. Ironically, it might well mean the faster depletion of resources. For, when all is said and done, the bottom line is that resources are limited.

Using the classical hare-tortoise race as a metaphor, Malthus suggested trying to "raise the quantity of provisions" even while working to slow down population growth—which is the essence of modern-day sustainable development.

It would be a foolish stretch of reason to believe that the earth can support 15 billion people or even more. The truth is staring at us right now from every corner of the world: countries are struggling to support even the current global population of nearly 6 billion. Eighty-six countries are currently classified as low-income food-deficient by the U.N. Food and Agricultural Organization. As many as 1.3 billion people—more than the combined population of Europe and North America—live in absolute poverty on the equivalent of one dollar or less per day. More than 840 million people are undernourished today, and even with all possible improvements in food production, there will still be at least 680 million undernourished people in the world in 2010.

While it may be easy for some of the critics from rich European or American nations to shed tears over falling fertility rates in Europe and discount the fears of overpopulation and its impact, it will be worthwhile to heed the cries of those poor overpopulated countries that suffer the painful, firsthand consequences of overpopulation. Their illiterate, impoverished millions, their overcrowded cities and parched farmlands can be transformed only by a concerted global conviction and effort.

Malthusian prophecy may not come true in this century or the next, but if we don't act now to stabilize population growth along the lines proposed at the 1994 International Conference on Population and Development it will be difficult to rule out that doomsday in the future. It will be in the world's interest to prove Malthus wrong. And Malthus would have welcomed it, as he suggested in the preface to his "Anonymous" first *Essay:*

> If he (the author) should succeed in drawing the attention of more able men to what he conceives to be the principal difficulty in the way to the improvement of society and should, in consequence, see this difficulty removed, even in theory, he will gladly retract his present opinions and rejoice in a conviction of his error.

"*Never have more people inhabited the world than today—and never before has food been so abundantly available.*"

Population Growth Does Not Threaten Global Resources

Nicholas Eberstadt

Nicholas Eberstadt argues in the following viewpoint that despite a human population explosion, the world's resources have actually increased. Eberstadt contends that unlike other species, humans can use problem-solving skills to expand resources. In fact, he maintains, people are actually consuming fewer natural resources as economies become knowledge- and skill-based. Moreover, according to Eberstadt, the population will probably peak around the year 2040 and then decline. Nicholas Eberstadt holds the Henry Wendt Chair in Political Economy at the American Enterprise Institute.

As you read, consider the following questions:
1. As reported by Eberstadt, by how much has the human lifespan increased since 1900?
2. Why does Eberstadt applaud the decrease in cereal prices over the last century?
3. How much of the world's total economic output is made up of services, as cited by the author?

Nicholas Eberstadt, "We've Lots of Room for People," *The American Enterprise*, vol. 11, December 2000, pp. 48–49. Copyright © 2000 by American Enterprise Institute for Public Policy Research. Reproduced by permission.

The notion that human beings, through their growing numbers and their escalating levels of consumption, are outstripping the globe's capacity to sustain them is one of the most powerful economic claims of the modern era. Ever since T.R. Malthus first made these arguments in a famous 1798 treatise, many people have been persuaded that a serious "population problem" is imminent and requires immediate action.

The durability of this notion is understandable, because it sounds so plausible. The planet, after all, is of a fixed size, and at some point a finite sphere will necessarily be unable to meet a geometrically rising demand upon its resources. Moreover, every other form of life on earth is governed by the immutable and unforgiving biological laws Malthus described: the regular tendency for a species to procreate beyond its environment's capacity to feed it, only to have its numbers brought back to "equilibrium" through brutal spikes in the death rate.

Humans Are Not Like Other Species

Yet human beings are not like other animals. Our species, unlike all others, can use problem-solving techniques to expand resources. Beasts cannot purposely transform their survival prospects. Human beings can—and they have done so dramatically, across the entire planet.

In 1900, the expected lifespan for men and women around the world probably averaged about 30 years. Today, according to projections by the U.N., it is probably over 65 years, and in the places conventionally deemed most prone to Malthusian calamity, improvements in longevity have been especially striking. During the past half-century, according to the U.N.'s figures, life expectancy for the low-income countries known as the "less developed regions" has jumped by well over 23 years, or more than half. During that same period, the overall infant mortality rate for the poorer countries is believed to have fallen by almost two-thirds. Humanity, in short, is in the midst of a "health explosion," which entirely accounts for the unprecedented "population explosion" of the twentieth century.

These tremendous and sustained worldwide improvements in human health speak to another crucial distinction between our species and all other animals. For the same factors that have made our health revolution possible—advances in scientific knowledge, the spread of education, improvements in organizational technique, and the like—have also supported a spectacular, and continuing, increase in human productivity.

A Food Revolution

Consider the race between population and food over the course of the twentieth century. Traditional Malthusian doctrine maintains that food production cannot keep pace with mankind's ability to multiply. The twentieth century should have provided a test case for that proposition, since between 1900 and 2000 the world's population nearly quadrupled, surging from perhaps 1.6 billion to over 6 billion.

Yet this extraordinary population explosion did not consign humanity to mounting hunger. Just the opposite: Mankind enjoys a far better diet today than it did when the earth's population was only one-fourth as large.

To be sure, millions upon millions of people still live under the threat of deadly hunger. Yet such tragic circumstances are now, finally, the distinct exception rather than the rule of the human condition. The inescapable fact is that humanity has never before been as well fed as today—and our improvements in nutritional well-being coincided with the most massive and rapid increase in population in human experience. In fact, despite our species' exponentially increasing demand for food, there is compelling evidence that foodstuffs are actually growing ever less scarce.

Falling Grain Prices

The nearby chart makes the point. It contrasts the twentieth century's global population trends with inflation-adjusted international price trends for corn, wheat, and rice. Real prices for each of these three cereals have plummeted by over 70 percent since 1900. These declines in prices were not smooth, but the temporary upswings in food costs were mainly the result of political disruptions—World War I, World War II, the Korean War, and the government-exacerbated "world food crisis" of the early 1970s—rather than environmental or demographic events.

The long-term fall in cereal prices is an important way to gauge the availability of food in the modern world. Since prices measure scarcity, falling prices mean foodstuffs are significantly less scarce at the end of the twentieth century than they were at its beginning—even though mankind is now consuming far more of them today.

Population vs. Grain Prices

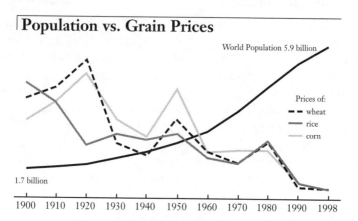

Commodity price indexes by Grilli and Yang, World Bank, and Plaffenzeller, University of Nottingham. Population from U.S. Bureau of the Census.

The facts are undeniable: Global population has been rising at an average pace of about 1.3 percent a year for a century, and global cereal prices have simultaneously been falling nearly 1.3 percent per year. Never have more people inhabited the world than today—and never before has food been so abundantly available.

A Growth in Global Resources

Faced with these incontestable data on the race between mouths and food, a sophisticated neo-Malthusian would retort that food is only one of many resources upon which people depend. And given our insatiable desire for expanding consumption, mankind's appetite for resources must eventually come into disastrous collision against some limiting natural constraint.

176

It is impossible today to disprove predictions about tomorrow, but the recent past does not comport with this vision of a world steadily denuded of resources by unchecked population growth and consumerism. Global natural resource constraints have actually been loosening in important areas. That paradox is illustrated by the contrast between global economic production and prices for primary commodities over the twentieth century.

The GDP estimates, prepared by eminent economic historian Angus Maddison, cover 56 countries that comprised almost 90 percent of the world's population and over 90 percent of the world's output as of 1992, and thus provide a reasonably close approximation to total global product. The primary commodity price index, developed by the economists Enzo R. Grilli and Maw Cheng Yang, takes the international cost of a market basket of 24 of the most commonly consumed "renewable and non-renewable resources"—foodstuffs, non-food agricultural goods, and metals—and adjusts for inflation. Maddison's estimates extend from 1900 to 1992; Grilli and Yang's, from 1900 to 1986. Both series are authoritative for the trends they depict.

Between 1900 and 1992, by Maddison's reckoning, global output grew at well over twice the pace of population growth, or at almost 3 percent a year. Between 1900 and 1992, this made for a 14-fold increase in the estimated planetary product. That means the global population's demand for goods and services also soared by a factor of 14.

But despite this staggering increase in demand, the relative price of non-fuel primary commodities dropped markedly. Between 1900 and 1986, the cumulative decline in the relative prices of these goods averaged –0.6 percent a year.

This primary commodity index excludes fuels. But adding oil and coal to the primary commodity market basket changes the picture only slightly. One Grilli and Yang series includes those two energy products, weighted to reflect their importance in overall trade. That particular series posts a cumulative decline of over 35 percent between 1900 and 1986, and trends downward at a pace of –0.5 percent per annum for those eight and a half decades.

Looking toward the future, Malthusians imagine that human demands upon a fragile planet are poised to rise indefinitely. Even this assumption may be wrong.

For one thing, patterns of economic activity around the globe have changed radically over the past century. As affluence has increased, the shares of overall output taken by agriculture and manufacturing—which draw heavily upon natural resources—have decreased, while the share accounted for by services has risen correspondingly. The World Bank estimates that services already make up over three-fifths of the world's total economic output. To an ever greater degree, modern economic growth is being driven by the demand for, and consumption of, human knowledge and skills rather than treasures extracted from the earth.

Second, it is far from certain that the human population will be growing in the coming millennium. In every industrial democracy in the contemporary world, fertility levels are now below the replacement level; in some of them, far below it. If continued, long-term population declines will result. Indeed, the proportion of humanity living in countries with fertility that will eventually yield population decline is rapidly approaching 50 percent. And for the rest of the world as well, fertility is falling steadily.

Reliable long-term population projections are impossible, since future birth rates are unknowable today. But if the pace of global fertility decline observed over the past 35 years were to continue for another quarter-century, human numbers would peak around the year 2040, and a world depopulation would commence thereafter.

None of this is to suggest that concern with humanity's current and prospective impact on the global environment is unwarranted. Quite the contrary. The case for conservation of, and stewardship over, natural resources is compelling. But responsible conservation and stewardship cannot be promoted by a worldview that strips mankind of its unique dignity, any more than the earth's "carrying capacity" for human beings can be established through rules and parameters derived from populations of fruit flies.

| *"Economic growth enables societies to advance in ways that are environmentally beneficial."*

Globalized Free Trade Will Protect Global Resources

James M. Sheehan

James M. Sheehan maintains in the following viewpoint that globalized free trade helps provide nations with the economic growth that makes environmental protection possible. According to Sheehan, richer individuals and governments are more willing to spend money to protect natural resources than are poorer ones. Sheehan claims that environmentalists are wrong to call for increased trade regulations to safeguard the environment because regulation restricts trade and thereby reduces the funds available for environmental protection. James M. Sheehan is director of international policy at the Competitive Enterprise Institute, a free-market think tank.

As you read, consider the following questions:
1. What is "eco-dumping," as defined by Sheehan?
2. According to the author, what environmental improvements have occurred in OECD countries since 1970?
3. What is the fundamental cause of pollution, in Sheehan's opinion?

"A more accurate name than the persuasive label 'free trade' is deregulated international commerce," scolds World Bank environmentalist Herman Daly. International regulation of trade is necessary "to build environmental responsibility into economic activity," and to assure that "trade meets the goals of environmentally sustainable development," in the words of Jay Hair, president of one of the largest environmental organizations in the United States, the National Wildlife Federation. As trade has become globalized, environmentalists argue, so has the magnitude of environmental degradation. "Further growth beyond the present scale is overwhelmingly likely to increase costs more rapidly than it increases benefits, thus ushering in a new era of 'uneconomic growth' that impoverishes rather than enriches," the foreboding Daly intones.

Environmentalist Opposition to Globalization

The "green" trade agenda necessarily entails greater political management and regulation of the private sector to safeguard social and environmental goals. In the eyes of environmental groups like the Worldwatch Institute, "trade can bring greater prosperity and improved quality of life, if properly managed, but if not it can become an engine of enormous destruction" of biodiversity, the global climate, and natural resources. Fearing destruction of the "global" environment, environmental groups call for radical alterations in the free-market system by government.

Environmental activists are particularly concerned with trade between progressive nations (with high regulatory standards) and more free-market or less developed countries (with lower regulatory standards). Nations without strict regulatory standards attract accelerated flows of international capital investment, leading to the creation of "pollution havens." The lack of stringent environmental regulation gives firms an unfair competitive trade advantage, amounting to an environmental subsidy which enables firms to undercut prices in export markets. This phenomenon is called environmental dumping, or "eco-dumping." Vice President Al Gore, in his bestselling *Earth in the Balance*, argues that "weak and ineffectual enforcement of pollution control measures should also be included in the definition of unfair trading practices."

The remedy for eco-dumping is a mixture of protectionism, industrial policy, and regulation. To offset the unfair cost advantages of another nation, a government can impose tariffs on the offending nation's imports (protectionism), or a government can subsidize the exports of its politically-preferred businesses (industrial policy). The purpose of import and export restrictions and subsidies is to induce nations to adopt stricter environmental standards, "internalizing" the externalized costs of unenlightened environmental policies. In this manner, nations can "harmonize" their trade-related regulations and risk assessment practices to facilitate an overall improvement in standards. Harmonization of production standards is envisioned as a means of establishing minimum environmental standards, either in the context of a regional trade agreement, or through a system of global environmental standards.

Environmentalist opposition to free trade stems from harsh scrutiny of "market failure" and the uncritical acceptance of political approaches to environmental protection. Wherever the market "fails" to protect environmental values to the desired degree, political intervention is assumed to be the solution. Because all economic activities have some impact on environmental quality, there is no end in sight for government intervention in the marketplace. Viewing economic growth as incompatible with a healthy environment, the environmental lobby insists on political restraints on private activity, both domestically and internationally. The environmentalist perspective is rapidly becoming conventional wisdom.

Richer Is Cleaner

Ultimately, however, there is no contradiction between a commercial free market and environmental quality. Numerous academic studies demonstrate a positive link between economic growth and environmental quality. Princeton University economists Gene M. Grossman and Alan B. Krueger have found that "economic growth tends to alleviate pollution problems once a country's per capita income reaches about $4,000 to $5,000 US dollars." In fact, levels of sulfur dioxide are significantly lower in countries that engage in significant international trade.

The link between economic growth and environmental improvement becomes clear in reviewing the ecological successes of the developed world. According to the World Bank, the economies of Organization for Economic Cooperation and Development (OECD) countries have grown by approximately 80 percent since 1970. During that time period, these countries have achieved nearly universal access to clean water supplies, sanitation, and waste disposal. Air quality has improved dramatically, with particulate emissions dropping by 60 percent and sulfur dioxide emissions by 38 percent. Pollution from large shipping accidents and oil spills has declined, and nearly all countries have increased the acreage of their forestlands. Similar statistics for the developing world demonstrate that improved environmental quality in all of these areas is generally associated with higher income.

What Is Globalization?

Globalization is about worldwide economic activity—about open markets, competition and the free flow of goods, services, capital and knowledge. Consumers are its principal beneficiary. Its benefits in terms of faster growth, quicker access to new technology, cheaper imports and greater competition are available for all. Globalization has made the world economy more efficient and has created hundreds of millions of jobs, mainly, but not only, in developing countries. It generates an upward spiral of jobs and prosperity for countries that embrace the process, although the advantages will not reach everybody at the same time.

Globalization is the name given to the accelerated pace at which markets and economies around the world have been integrating during the past 20 years. It is driven essentially—but not solely—by free trade, capital mobility and rapid technological progress. The benefits of this greater openness—faster growth, quick access to new technologies, cheaper imports, greater competition—are too easily taken for granted. It has brought considerable benefits to countries that have embraced the process and has the potential to add further to growth and prosperity in all countries.

International Chamber of Commerce, November 22, 2000.

There are a variety of reasons for the beneficial relationship between growth and environmental quality. As economic activity increases, so does human interaction with nature. Since most human actions strive to improve quality of life, environmental amenities receive greater attention. Environmental improvements are particularly significant in market-oriented economies. The societal institutions that facilitate prosperity, such as property rights, market-based prices, and overall economic freedom, are equally essential for raising environmental quality. These institutions form the bulwark of private stewardship of natural resources and, thus, sustainable management practices. Market forces naturally drive economies to become more efficient by reducing the costs associated with energy and materials use, and waste disposal. Moreover, since growth creates wealth, greater economic resources are made available to address the primary human needs, which must be fulfilled before individuals will focus on environmental amenities. According to Marian Radetski, an economist at the University of Luleo in Sweden, "rich consumers are more willing than poor ones to spend substantial parts of their income for safeguarding high environmental standards."

Furthermore, poverty is a significant cause of environmental degradation. Poorer people are more likely to exploit environmental commons in search of fuelwood and other basic necessities, causing overhunting, overfishing, and stress to water resources. Lacking significant employment opportunities and productive land, the poor in the Third World often must utilize marginal lands for food production, attempting to farm in deserts or tropical forests. The result is environmental degradation in the form of soil erosion, desertification, and deforestation.

Moreover, economic growth enables societies to advance in ways that are environmentally beneficial. At earlier stages of development, pollution problems are likely to be more threatening to human beings. Air- and water-borne hazards can result in immediate illness or death. As societies advance, pollution problems decline in severity. Environmental concerns generally become less life-threatening, and more aesthetic in nature.

The Folly of Government Regulation

Even though growth coincides with environmental improvement, "market failure" is often blamed for the existence of pollution itself. Many environmentalists consider the system of capitalism and private enterprise inherently responsible for environmental externalities. Only government regulation in the public interest can force businesses to internalize social costs, according to this argument, and such regulation must be extended to trade. Thus, there is a strong anti-market bias to environmentalist arguments.

The market-failure argument leads inexorably to central planning; any human activity with environmental impacts must be politically controlled. Government is entrusted to effectively foster only the types of economic growth which are environmentally friendly, while preventing the types that are not. Yet no government has the capability of assimilating the vast amounts of economic, technological, and scientific data necessary to make such determinations. The task of ecological central planning is no easier than economic central planning.

If market failure was truly the cause of pollution, we would expect the absence of markets in the centrally-planned economies of Eastern Europe would have been environmentally beneficial. On the contrary, without the profit motive of the market, some of the worst environmental degradation in the world occurred in the former Soviet Bloc. Central planning failed largely because it could not efficiently distribute resources. Neither could it safeguard environmental resources. Data from sample market and socialist economies shows that market economies become more resource-efficient with economic growth. Socialist countries, however, are generally more resource intensive, even in times of recession. Without a profit motive, there is little incentive for political owners of a resource to conserve for the future in order to maximize returns.

Free Markets Are Truly Green

In a market economy, environmental and other costs are internalized more thoroughly via the price system. Internalization is made possible by the extension of property rights and a system of voluntary exchange to an ever-wider array of resources. As environmental and other resources are integrated into the market system of voluntary exchange, information is conveyed through prices, which encourages more creative resolutions of environmental and other problems. Falling prices for energy and raw materials demonstrate that the market's technological improvements and efficiency gains are making resources more abundant.

The "market failure" argument misses the fundamental cause of pollution—the lack of private property institutions. Individuals are far more likely to care for the environmental sustainability of their own resources. Logically, the less common property there is, the less pollution will be tolerated by a society of individual property owners. Likewise, by internalizing external costs, market forces obviate the need for corrective regulations. By reducing the scope of government intervention, markets enable individuals to seek redress from those who impose unwanted pollution costs. Political owner/managers are incapable of seeking adequate redress primarily because they cannot calculate accurate prices and values for environmental amenities. Thus, a free market effectively implements the "polluter pays principle," making capitalism the only form of sustainable development. Pollution externalities could be reduced further by eliminating the remaining barriers to full private property rights.

More to Fear from Protectionism

Environmentalists need not fear that expansion of trade will produce growth in pollution. To the extent that expanded trade is generating economic growth, environmental quality should also improve. This fundamental economic reality does not change simply because goods and services are crossing borders. The same free-market institutions which generate economic gains also generate environmental gains. To the extent that protective tariffs and subsidies restrict and distort trade, they reduce income and, hence, the demand for environmental quality.

Environmentalists have more to fear from protectionism. Current agricultural policies cause major distortions of world food production and trade. Industrial countries encourage agricultural production with price supports and other subsidies totaling $200 billion per year, while developing countries discourage agricultural production through tax and trade policies. Agricultural subsidies in the United States, for example, are responsible for intense chemical pesticide and fertilizer use on farmlands. By fostering inefficient land use, US subsidies and land set-aside programs contribute to soil erosion and loss of wetlands and forests. Federal mismanagement also encourages farmers to overplant while discouraging crop rotation, depleting soils and exacerbating pest eradication. By scaling back interventionist government policies, trade liberalization would have significant environmental benefits.

"Environmental damage can be a by-product of globalization and trade liberalization."

Globalized Free Trade Can Exhaust Global Resources

Stanley Wood

According to Stanley Wood in the following viewpoint, trade liberalization and globalization can adversely affect the environment, especially in developing nations. Wood argues that as poor nations are pressured to produce goods for the global marketplace, they will increasingly exploit their natural resources and degrade the environment. Unfortunately, he contends, the infusion of wealth such countries eventually gain from increased trade will come too late to mitigate the damage. Stanley Wood is a senior scientist in the Environment and Production Technology Division at the International Food Policy Research Institute.

As you read, consider the following questions:
1. As defined by the author, what is the "inverted-U" phenomenon?
2. What are "pollution havens," according to Wood?
3. In the author's opinion, what might be the effects of global climate change on developing nations?

Globalization affects the environment in several ways. It changes the structure and pace of economic growth and, hence, the scale and nature of resource consumption and waste emission. It also fosters the creation of regulatory frameworks and institutions for promoting trade, the flow of capital, and the diffusion of technology, in ways that can exacerbate or mitigate environmental impacts. Environmental impacts may be felt locally, affecting those who earn their livelihood by exploiting resources such as land, water, and biodiversity. Or they may be felt further afield, through broader effects on natural ecosystems, the freshwater cycle, the ozone layer, nutrient flows, the climate, and so on. There are thus sound economic as well as humanitarian and ethical reasons to map the impacts of globalization on the environment.

Evidence supports the notion that open and transparent economies are more likely to be prosperous. Yet measures of prosperity rarely account for environmental costs of production. Some argue that depletion of natural resources, pollution of air, water, and soil, loss of biodiversity, and global warming significantly reduce and in some circumstances outweigh the growth-related benefits of globalization. Furthermore, economic and environmental costs and benefits may not be equitably distributed if the lion's share of economic benefits from globalization accrues to developed countries, while the developing world shoulders the environmental burdens.

Environment, Growth, and Competitiveness

Trade generates economic benefits because, given free and efficient markets, it encourages trading partners to specialize in goods or services they have some comparative advantage in. Since developing countries often have abundant natural resources and cheap, plentiful labor, trade liberalization has fostered shifts toward labor and resource-intensive sectors such as mining, logging, garment manufacturing, and export crop production. Most of these sectors, however, generate significant environmental "externalities." These are environmental costs not reflected in the production costs of individual enterprises, be they farm households or multinational companies. The results of ignoring the true social costs of production are excessive production, resource consumption, and waste emission.

Proponents of globalization argue that many environmental problems can be countered by stimulating economic growth. A portion of the overall economic gain can be transferred to individuals and communities affected by environmental degradation. Investments can be made to strengthen environmental institutions, and cleaner, more resource-efficient technologies can be developed and adopted. Based on studies of developed countries, proponents also point to the so-called "inverted-U" phenomenon. That is, although natural resource consumption and degradation increase as economies grow, an income threshold is attained above which demand for a better environment stimulates investment in environmental protection and rehabilitation. Degradation is thus reduced. Many developing countries, however, are so poor, population growth so high, and natural resources already so stressed, that catastrophic, perhaps irreversible, environmental damage may well occur long before any such threshold is reached.

Although environmental damage can be a by-product of globalization and trade liberalization, incentives for addressing its underlying causes are mixed. While developing countries suffer the greatest damage, they are also under the greatest pressure to accelerate economic growth to increase incomes and combat poverty. And since environmental policies and institutions are likely to be weak in developing countries, producers there (be they domestic or foreign) have little incentive to care about the environmental externalities of their actions. Rampant logging of the world's biodiversity- and carbon-rich tropical forests, for example, testifies to this. This raises concerns that globalization might create "pollution havens" in developing countries, where foreign investors operate to escape stricter environmental laws and enforcement in their own countries. There are also fears that governments might progressively push environmental standards lower as they compete to attract scarce foreign investment (the "race to the bottom" hypothesis). Available evidence suggests that such fears might be overstated. Foreign investors are generally much more concerned with factors such as wage rates, available infrastructure, and the repatriation of earnings.

Some governments' adoption of lenient environmental standards raises concerns that these countries are, in effect, subsidizing exports and reducing the competitiveness of producers in countries with stricter standards. Attempts to raise environmental standards bring protests from domestic producers who are concerned about potentially higher production costs and loss of international competitiveness. Politicians express concern too about increasing domestic prices in the face of widespread poverty. Furthermore, developing countries maintain that differences in resource endowment, pollution assimilation capacities, and social preferences with regard to environmental standards are legitimate sources of their comparative advantage. Attempting to reconcile such conflicting interests poses enormous challenges to environmental policymakers.

Global Environmental Concerns

Despite the political and technical difficulties involved, the international community has proven willing to take collective action to address environmental issues of global concern. International initiatives have been mounted on climate change (United Nations Framework Convention on Climate Change), movements of hazardous waste (the Basel Convention), biodiversity loss (Convention on Biological Diversity), trade in endangered species (Convention on International Trade in Endangered Species of Wild Fauna and Flora [CITES]), ozone layer depletion (the Montreal Protocol), desertification (United Nations Convention to Combat Desertification), and loss of wetlands (the Ramsar Convention on Wetlands). While it is not clear that globalization per se has been a dominant factor in creating the problems these initiatives address, some do relate to trade and some are likely exacerbated by trade liberalization. There is thus a growing sentiment that formal linkages should be strengthened between the World Trade Organization (WTO) process and global environmental regulation. But obstacles remain, such as resentment toward rich countries seeking to impose standards that are at odds with economic conditions and social preferences in poor countries. Moves to strengthen environmental regulation as a pre-condition for trade are perceived largely as a guise by which rich countries legitimize nontariff trade barriers.

The Battle over Fresh Water

One would expect governments and global bureaucracies to advocate water conservation. Instead what's being proposed is to privatize, commodify, and globalize the planet's remaining fresh water—its lakes, rivers, streams—to sell exploitation rights to corporations, and let the global market decide who gets to drink it or use it. Most of the water goes to industrial users once water systems are fully privatized and globalized—a process that is being massively aided by the new General Agreement on Trade in Services (GATS), as well as the Free Trade Area of the Americas (FTAA). Most of the people on the planet who are actually thirsty, will not be able to pay for it. Who gets the scarce water—Bill Gates or the peasants in Bolivia?

Jerry Mander, *IFG Bulletin*, Summer 2002.

Climate change is one of the most controversial global issues. Although there are many uncertainties, studies suggest that much of the world will be impacted increasingly by climate change linked to human-induced emission of greenhouse gases. Not only are mean temperatures likely to rise, but also the incidence and severity of extreme events such as heat spells, droughts, and floods are expected to increase. Projected climate change will not affect all countries equally however. Global agricultural production appears to be sustainable in the aggregate, but impacts on crop and livestock productivity will vary considerably across regions. Successive studies suggest that temperate areas (largely richer countries) stand to increase their agricultural potential while that of many tropical and subtropical areas will decline. The poorest countries in Sub-Saharan Africa (already a hot region with large tracts of arid or semiarid land) appear to be the most vulnerable to temperature increases and changing rainfall patterns. Countries in South and Southeast Asia could be affected by increasing irregularity and intensity of tropical storms. The Pacific Island nations could suffer losses of coastal land due to rising sea level, saltwater intrusion into water supplies, and increased damage from tropical storms. The anticipated disproportionate impact of climate change on the poorest countries means the number of people at risk of hunger is also projected to rise, compared to a baseline without climate change.

Forces for Change

Asymmetries exist not only in the likely environmental impacts of globalization on developed versus developing countries, but also in the capacity of countries to mitigate or adapt to change or to seek compensation. Most developing countries have only limited mechanisms by which communities can seek redress when confronted with environmental externalities like water pollution and increased flooding caused by activities upstream, or the loss of food and fuelwood due to forest conversion. But externalities may also have consequences far beyond the location of production. When externalities "spill" across borders, such as greenhouse gas emissions, ozone layer depletion, and biodiversity loss—particularly extinction of species—the full force of international environmental advocacy is often mobilized. Global grassroots activism now has a significant influence on international trade dialogues, including their environmental aspects.

Recent developments in information and communication technology are also shaping the debate on globalization and the environment. The Internet and email are powerful tools for sharing information among global communities, including scientists, the private sector, policy analysts, community leaders, and environmental activists. Information on best practices, technology, institutional innovations, and specific environmental incidents can be relayed rapidly the world over in photos, text, web links, and sound bites. The enhanced flow of information is proving particularly valuable to environmental advocacy and action groups in developing countries. Access to information hitherto unavailable nationally strengthens the capability of such organizations, often nongovernmental organizations (NGOs), to raise awareness and promote national debate on the plight of the environment and the people whose livelihoods depend on it.

Mobilization of informal collective action in developing countries is also proving effective. While studies of firm behavior in developed countries cite regulatory pressure as the most potent driver of environmentally preferred technical change, similar studies in developing countries find community pressure to be the predominant force. Increasingly too, the policies and practices of multinational enterprises in developing countries are shaped by (fear of) adverse media campaigns mounted by international NGOs aimed at developed-country consumers and investors.

The Need for a Concerted Global Effort

Global environmental issues, ranging from depletion of natural resources and biodiversity to climate change, are complex. Analyses of future trends are cloaked in uncertainties, given our limited understanding of earth systems and their interactions with changing economic and social conditions. Population growth, shifting consumption patterns, and institutional innovation will undoubtedly continue to affect the environment, as will the pace and nature of technical change. There is reason to believe that these changes will hasten the deterioration of environmental conditions faced by already vulnerable populations in developing countries. Such deterioration would likely reinforce vicious cycles of humanitarian crises, conflict over resources, and lack of development. To confront these pressing environmental challenges, a concerted global effort is needed with rich countries taking the lead and prepared to adopt a truly global vision.

"We must find ways to diminish environmental degradation caused by human production and consumption activities."

Sustainable Development Is Necessary to Protect Global Resources

Danja Van Der Veldt

In the following viewpoint, Danja Van Der Veldt asserts that sustainable development—meeting the needs of the present generation without compromising the ability of future generations to meet their own needs—is the only effective way to reverse environmental destruction and resource depletion. She argues that the price of goods should reflect the environmental costs associated with their manufacture and disposal, and contends that environmentally destructive products such as automobiles should be taxed more heavily. Van Der Veldt maintains that in order for sustainable development to succeed, people must begin to treat the earth with respect. Danja Van Der Veldt was a research scientist at the Scientific Institute for Environmental Management at the Faculty for Economics and Econometrics of the University of Amsterdam.

As you read, consider the following questions:
1. As reported by the author, what are the five types of indirect benefits derived from environmental resources?
2. What is the difference between the PPP and the UPP, according to the author?

Danja Van Der Veldt, "Future Perfect," *Forum for Applied Research and Public Policy*, vol. 14, Winter 1999, pp. 13–15, 18–19. Copyright © 1999 by *Forum for Applied Research and Public Policy*. Reproduced by permission.

O ur world is in trouble. The environment is under siege, and the Earth's resources are being depleted at an alarming rate. Acid rain, air and water pollution, deforestation, desertification, flooding, global warming, hazardous wastes, loss of biodiversity, ozone depletion, water shortages, wetlands destruction—the list goes on and on—are all part of a malaise that is robbing us of our future. . . .

Defining Terms

In 1987, in response to these and other concerns, the World Commission on Environment and Development published *Our Common Future*, which lays the foundation for our current understanding of sustainable development. This document, also known as the "Brundtland Report," recognizes that the present generation, through its use of natural resources and environmental services, is borrowing from future generations with no repayment plan. Sustainable development may represent the only option we have for paying back this loan.

Sustainable development, as defined in the Brundtland Report, is "development that meets the needs of the present generation without compromising the ability of future generations to meet their own needs." For development to be sustainable, the report concludes, three elements—environmental, economic, and social development—must all be present.

The World Bank also believes that sustainable development must be based on environmental, economic, and social elements. The World Bank argues, though, that the meaning of *needs* in the Brundtland definition of sustainable development is vague. How, for example, do you compare the needs of the poor in developing countries with the needs of the wealthy in industrialized countries? Moreover, how can you possibly anticipate what future generations will need?

On this matter, the World Bank deviates from the Brundtland Report and suggests that the goal of sustainability is "to leave future generations as many opportunities as, if not more than, we have had ourselves." To accomplish this goal, according to the World Bank, our stock of "capital" must grow.

The World Bank uses the term *capital* in its broadest sense to include not only produced assets, such as houses, roads, and factories, but also natural resources and human resources, including labor, investments in education and health care, and the cultural institutions that enable society to function.

Getting There from Here

Meeting the goals of the World Bank and the Brundtland Report will require significant shifts in the way we operate. Specifically, we must find ways to diminish environmental degradation caused by human production and consumption activities. These shifts must engender economic, technological, and sociodemographic change. They must also penetrate the realms of education, media and politics, and ethics and spirituality.

To obtain the best results in the movement toward sustainable development, we must take action simultaneously in these areas. For example, we should remove fuel subsidies while educating people about the damaging environmental effects their automobiles cause. At the same time, we should also be providing them with alternative transportation solutions.

The areas of change can be mutually supportive; a change in one area can have positive spillover effects in other areas. For instance, removal of electricity subsidies will give people an incentive to invest in energy efficient technologies. And in some cases, state-of-the art technology, in turn, can actually reduce consumption.

Green Accounting

Traditional frameworks used for measuring national income and wealth do not recognize the real costs of environmental depletion and pollution. National income—or gross national product—measures must be adjusted to reflect environmental degradation. When calculating the economic value of a natural resource, one must consider direct benefits derived from physical use of an environmental resource, such as the health benefits of clean water or the recreational benefits of visiting a national park.

Indirect benefits, obtained from environmental resources without directly using or visiting them, should also be taken into account. Ismael Serageldin, from the World Bank, identifies five types of indirect benefits:

- Existence value—the knowledge that an environmental service exists, such as carbon dioxide uptake by trees.
- Vicarious value—indirect consumption of an environmental resource through, for example, books or movies that depict environmental themes.
- Option value—opportunity to use the resource at some future date.
- Quasi-option value—the possibility of future technologies or knowledge enhancing the value of a natural resource, such as the discovery of new medicines from tropical rainforest plants.
- Bequest value—the benefit that the current generation obtains from preserving the environment for future generations.

The economic value of natural resources has to be estimated because accurately measuring direct and indirect environmental benefits is essentially impossible. One method is to ask individuals how much they would be willing to pay for some environmental resource or change in resource status. For instance, how much extra would you pay for a new type of engine that greatly reduces auto emissions but does not alter driving performance?

Another approach is to estimate the value of a recreation site by analyzing the travel expenditures of visitors to that site. A third method uses the variation of property values to estimate the value of local environmental quality.

By applying these and other methods, we can identify a country as being sustainable if it accumulates capital faster than it depletes its present stock—in other words, if it provides future generations with as much, if not more, capital per person than we have ourselves. And, of course, capital is used here in its broadest sense—the way the World Bank defines it—to include human and natural resources as well as traditional capital, such as factories, highways, and tools.

To achieve sustainable development, the World Bank emphasizes the importance of investments in education, which will increase capital stock. In developing countries, income derived from natural resources should be invested foremost in fostering human capabilities. In 1960, for example, Pakistan and Korea had similar incomes but significantly different rates of primary school enrollment. In Korea, this rate was 94 percent, while in Pakistan it was 30 percent. During the next 25 years, the per capita gross domestic product of Korea grew to three times that of Pakistan.

The Effects of Pricing

The traditional way of coping with environmental degradation has been to impose environmental regulations. These command-and-control measures, however, are often not the most cost-effective methods for reaching environmental goals. A more effective approach is to adjust the prices of goods and services to reflect real economic, social, and environmental costs associated with pollution and extraction of natural resources. That way, the costs of environmental degradation can be fully integrated into the production and consumption decisions throughout the economy.

The polluter pays principle (PPP) and the user pays principle (UPP) offer two avenues for achieving this integration. The PPP, adopted by the Organization for Economic Cooperation and Development (OECD) in 1972, forces the polluter to bear the expenses of preventing and controlling pollution. The UPP, which has not officially been accepted by the OECD, seeks to have the price of a natural resource reflect the total costs involved in using it.

Economic instruments—among them subsidies, taxes, and tradeable emissions rights—can efficiently be used to adjust prices and internalize external environmental costs. One benefit of using economic instruments for environmental purposes is that they can generate a double dividend by decreasing pollution while boosting government income. The extra revenue obtained from higher taxes on environmentally harmful activities, for example, can be used to lower taxes on income from such constructive activities as work, savings, and investment.

Moreover, the revenue can be used to compensate those who are most burdened by increased prices—primarily the poor and small businesses. For instance, if water prices in an area of water scarcity are increased, the government could use the extra money to help small farmers pay for more efficient irrigation methods, such as drip irrigation systems.

Another important advantage of using economic instruments to achieve environmental goals is that they give consumers and producers an economic incentive—for example, through higher energy prices—to invest in environmentally beneficial technologies, such as energy-efficient machinery.

Taxes Should Equal Harm

Ideally, the PPP would entail setting an environmental tax that is equivalent to the environmental degradation associated with the manufacture, use, and disposal of a product. While in practice, calculating this optimal price level is often difficult, increasing prices slightly to achieve some decrease in environmental degradation marks a worthwhile start.

Environmental taxes are used widely and successfully in industrialized countries. In developing countries, however, their use is not as common, because it is difficult to increase prices of natural resources when standards of living are low. Instead, developing countries often subsidize the use of natural resources such as water and fuels. Globally, in fact, nations spend US$700 billion or more each year on subsidies for energy, water, road transportation, and agriculture.

Some of these subsidies stimulate an excessive rate of pollution and depletion of natural resources, however, and often do not serve their original goal of achieving social welfare. As a consequence, such subsidies have proven to be unsustainable and should be eliminated. Case studies from Malaysia, Indonesia, Ghana, Zimbabwe, Colombia, and Turkey showed that increasing energy prices during the 1980s to eliminate subsidies did not harm the welfare of the poor nor hamper growth, inflation, or industrial competitiveness. At the same time, revenues, generated from these energy price increases, improved.

Another study of economic instruments as tools for sustainable energy consumption in Costa Rica proposed levying environmental taxes on fuels in the transportation sector and on electricity in the highest income brackets. The revenues obtained through these economic instruments would have been substantial and could have been used to compensate the poor for marginal losses incurred, mostly through higher diesel prices, which translated into higher costs for public transportation. Moreover, the revenues could have been invested in environmentally beneficial projects such as reforestation and improved public transportation systems and roads.

This study also found, however, that increasing fuel prices would not significantly decrease fuel demand nor significantly reduce pollution caused by the use of fuels. To bolster the effects of increased fuel prices, environmental taxes should be accompanied by such regulations as energy efficiency standards as well as wide-reaching educational programs. These and other initiatives could be financed with government revenues generated through increased fuel prices.

The Ethics of Sustainability

A substantial environmental ethic must be involved in any sustainability initiative. For example, Anglican Archbishop John Taylor asked, "Is it immoral that the United States has to import over one half of its energy supply?" Similarly, he asks, "Is it reasonable that a child born in the United States or immigrating to it at an early age will probably consume 30 to 40 times the energy and natural resources per capita compared to the rest of the world, and possibly 200 times as much as some of the poorest underdeveloped countries?" One common belief among those few members of the general public who have given some casual thought to sustainable use of the planet is that, by minor changes in present practices, sustainability can be achieved without substantive behavioral change. However, much of the early literature on sustainable use of the planet indicates that a major paradigm shift and fundamental changes in human behavior, ethics, and lifestyles will be necessary.

John Cairns Jr., *Environmental Health Perspectives*, November 1997.

Human behavior is influenced by values, world views, ethics, religion, and spirituality. To achieve a more sustainable world, many of our current beliefs will need to change. During past centuries, we have moved from a world where natural capital was abundant and human-made capital remained the limiting factor, to a world where natural capital has become the limiting factor.

In realizing this approach to caring for the Earth, ethical change and spiritual reflection become essential. Many philosophers and spiritual leaders have argued that we are part of a moral order that extends beyond us to other creatures on Earth. Some even see the Earth itself as a living and finite system in which humans operate as a part of nature rather than apart from it.

Many traditional religions have taught humans to treat the Earth with respect and care. While these religions have lost ground today, ecological spirituality and ethics might be able to build common ground for creating a universal respect for the Earth. Ecological spirituality would be based on viewing human beings as part of the Earth and on encouraging us to interrelate with the environment respectfully, in ways that will not harm the larger ecosystem.

Environmental ethics, which is based on this same notion, seeks to inspire people to accept the need for greater equity between the wealthy and poor. This tenet is an essential requirement for a sustainable world. Introducing environmental ethics into major areas of study in high school and university programs around the world therefore would be a worthwhile endeavor.

Environmental degradation and social inequity are major worldwide concerns. It has taken the human species centuries to create the environmental problems we now face. It will likely take us decades, if not longer, to correct them so we can achieve sustainable development. An emphasis on environmental education, effective use of the media and politics, and increased concern for ethics can help immensely to heighten public awareness of environmental degradation and ways to reverse it. To that end, individuals must take responsibility for their contribution to the problem and learn how their daily activities affect environmental health.

Meanwhile, government and community support—through financial incentives and investments in environmentally beneficial projects and technologies—are crucial for changing producer and consumer behaviors.

All of us—consumers, manufacturers, policymakers—have played a role in despoiling the Earth. A unified, global effort that enlists the help and goodwill of all of us will be necessary to save the Earth and nudge us along the path to sustainability.

"The wealth created by exploiting resources is often more beneficial than the wealth preserved by 'banking' those resources for future use."

Sustainable Development Is Unnecessary

Jerry Taylor

Jerry Taylor argues in the following viewpoint that the concept of sustainable development—meeting the needs of the present without compromising the ability of future generations to meet their own needs—is misguided. For one thing, he asserts, the idea of preserving resources is problematic because resources are not static; they change as people develop technology to extract and process them. Moreover, Taylor contends that exploiting resources as opposed to conserving them creates wealth that is passed on to future generations, a phenomenon that has resulted in increasingly higher living standards for people throughout the world. Jerry Taylor is director of natural resource studies at the Cato Institute and senior editor of *Regulation* magazine.

As you read, consider the following questions:
1. What is the "strong" definition of sustainable development, as defined by Taylor?
2. According to the author, how has the resource assessment of uranium changed over the last century?
3. How is the concept of sustainable development related to the issue of abortion, in the author's opinion?

The mantra of "sustainable development" is constantly on the lips of the international agencies and non-governmental organizations helping lesser-developed countries. The concept seems innocuous enough; after all, who would favor "unsustainable development"? But the fundamental premise of the idea—that economic growth, if left unconstrained and unmanaged by the state, threatens unnecessary harm to the environment and may prove economically ephemeral—is dubious. Indeed, the policy prescriptions that are generally endorsed by those concerned about sustainable development are inimical to our best environmental and economic interests. This is so for three reasons:

• If economic growth were to be slowed or stopped, it would be impossible to improve environmental conditions.

• The bias for command-and-control regulations on the part of those endorsing the concept of sustainable development will only serve to make environmental protection more expensive; hence, we have to "purchase" less of it.

• Strict pursuit of sustainable development, as many environmentalists mean it, would only do violence to the welfare of future generations.

The debate surrounding sustainable development is important because it advertises itself as a comprehensive governing philosophy for the twenty-first century. Indeed, Vice President Al Gore has called the need for environmental protection the best "central organizing principle" of the modern state. This is heavy stuff. It puts sustainable development in the pantheon of other "central organizing principles" proposed for the state over the years—such as rule by class or race and absolute rule by majority. While environmental protection is certainly important, making it the government's chief principle would concentrate tremendous power in the hands of those who believe only they can best direct human affairs. The results of such experiments have been less than spectacular and usually counterproductive, to say the least.

What Is Sustainable Development?

Despite its institutionalization, sustainable development is rather difficult to define coherently. The United Nations

Commission on Economic Development (UNCED), in its landmark 1987 report, *Our Common Future*, defines it as that which "meets the needs of the present without compromising the ability of future generations to meet their own needs." But that definition is hopelessly problematic. How can we be reasonably expected to know, for instance, what the needs of people in 2100 might be? Moreover, one way people typically "meet their own needs" is by spending money on food, shelter, education, and whatever else they deem necessary or important. Is sustainable development, then, simply a euphemism for the creation of wealth (which, after all, is handed down to our children for their subsequent use)? True, there are human needs—such as peace, freedom, and individual contentment—that cannot be met simply by material means, but sustainable-development advocates seldom dwell on the importance of those nonmaterial, non "resource-based" psychological needs when discussing the concept.

Thus, sophisticated proponents of sustainable development are forced to discard as functionally meaningless the UNCED definition. Otherwise, the UNCED definition can be read as a call for society to maximize human welfare over time. An entire profession has grown up around that proposition. It is known as economics, and maximizing human welfare is known not as "sustainable development" but as "optimality." Can it really be that Adam Smith's *The Wealth of Nations* was the world's first call for sustainable development?

Economists David Pearce and Jeremy Warford, two of the world's more serious thinkers about sustainable development, disclose that by sustainable development, many advocates mean "a process in which the natural-resource base is not allowed to deteriorate." This is generally known as the "strong" definition of sustainability. The "weak" definition allows the natural-resource base to deteriorate as long as biological resources are maintained at a minimum critical level and the wealth generated by the exploitation of natural resources is preserved for future generations, which is otherwise "robbed" of their rightful inheritance. Weak sustainability, then, can be thought of as "the amount of consumption that can be sustained indefinitely without degrading capital stocks."

Unfortunately, both "strong" and "weak" definitions of sustainable development pose problems as well. As Robert Hahn of the American Enterprise Institute points out, the narrower the definition, the easier it is to pin down, but the less satisfactory the concept. That does not, however, reduce the concept's utility as (in the description of the Competitive Enterprise Institute's James Sheehan) "an overarching political philosophy merging the twin goals of conservation and controlled economic development."

The Pitfalls of "Strong" Sustainability

What is "the natural-resource base" we are directed not to draw down? Resources are simply those assets that can be used profitably for human benefit. "Natural" resources, then, are a subset of the organic and inorganic material we think of as constituting the biological "environment," since not all of that material can be used profitably.

What can be used productively by man changes with time, technology, and material demand. Waves, for example, are not harnessed for human benefit today and thus cannot really be thought of as a "natural resource." But the technology to harness the movement of waves to generate energy certainly exists, and the day when the cost of doing so is lower than the cost of alternative energy sources is the day when waves become a "natural resource." Uranium, to cite another example, would not have been considered a resource a century ago, but is most certainly thought of as such today. Petroleum was not an important resource 100 years ago, but today is thought of as perhaps the most important one to modern society.

Thus, what is and is not part of any society's "natural-resource base" changes. Conserving today's base does not ensure that tomorrow's is secure, and drawing down today's does not necessarily mean that tomorrow's is in jeopardy.

Moreover, the relative abundance of a society's natural resources can change dramatically with technological advance. For example, there are 6,784 trillion fewer barrels of oil in the ground today than there were in 1981, the year in which relative oil scarcity was greatest. At first glance, then, one might think that the natural-resource base has deteriorated.

Yet oil is more abundant today than it was 17 years ago. After adjusting for inflation, the price of a barrel of Saudi crude has declined by 62 percent and U.S. crude by 64 percent since 1980. The reasons for this increased oil abundance are several-fold. First, new technologies have emerged that make oil discovery and production far more efficient and thus less costly. Second, greater efficiency in using resources (a reaction to previous run-ups in petroleum prices as well as ongoing technological advances) has helped reduce the amount of oil necessary to produce a unit of goods or services and, hence, the relative abundance of the energy-resource base. Indeed, according to the U.S. Energy Department's Energy Information Administration, the amount of petroleum and natural gas necessary to produce a dollar's worth of GDP has declined by 29 percent since 1980. The story is not unique to petroleum; all resources have become far more abundant— not more scarce—throughout the twentieth century (and indeed, throughout recorded history).

If sustainable development, then, is understood as an admonition that the aggregate size of the natural-resource base (absent any consideration of demand) should "not be allowed to deteriorate," then it is not particularly helpful. It posits wrongly that absolute (as opposed to relative) scarcity is the primary threat to the economy and human society at large. And the theory is oblivious to the ongoing process of resource creation. As economists Harold Barnett and Chandler Morse explained in their classic work, *Scarcity and Growth*, as resources become more scarce, people will anticipate future scarcities, prices will be bid up, incentives will be created for developing new technologies and substitutes, and the resource base will be renewed.

Wild-Eyed Optimism?

Is Barnett and Morse's optimism regarding "just in time" delivery of new technologies and resource subsidies justified? Well, historical experience would certainly seem to justify their optimism. Those who find the theory counterintuitive betray a fundamental misunderstanding of the genesis of resources. Natural resources do not exist independent of man and are not materials we simply find and then exploit like buried treasure. On the contrary, they are created by mankind. As resource economist Thomas De Gregori points out, "humans are the active agent, having ideas that they use to transform the environment for human purposes. . . . Resources are not fixed and finite because they are not natural. They are a product of human ingenuity resulting from the creation of technology and science."

The late David Osterfeld thus concluded that "since resources are a function of human knowledge and our stock of knowledge has increased over time, it should come as no surprise that the stock of physical resources has also been expanding." Obsessing on conserving present resources is akin to a farmer obsessing over conserving eggs rather than the chickens that lay them.

High Growth = Environmental Benefits

Economist Seth Norton (1998) of Wheaton College has studied the relationship between nations' rates of growth (not their income levels) and environmental quality. Norton defines high-growth countries as those with annual rates of growth of over 4.5 percent and low-growth countries as those with growth rates under 1 percent. Norton found that high growth is correlated with environmental benefits. For example, he found that over 84 percent of people in high-growth countries had access to safe drinking water, while only 53 percent in low-growth countries did. Eighty-three percent of the people in high-growth countries had access to proper sanitation while only 40 percent did in low-growth countries. Life expectancy was 63 years in high-growth countries but only 50 years in low-growth countries.

Matthew Brown and Jane S. Shaw, *PERC Reports*, February 1999.

The sustainable-development imperative betrays an ill-considered bias for natural as opposed to man-made capital. In truth, the wealth created by exploiting resources is often more beneficial than the wealth preserved by "banking" those resources for future use. Daniel Boggs has criticized the "rhetoric [that] says we didn't inherit from our parents, we are borrowing from our children."

Argues Boggs: "This is usually designed to make us ashamed to use anything. Logically, it should also make us hate our parents for using up some of 'our' oil, or iron, or whatever. Yet, our parents did build this world for us." He went on to point out that previous generations "created the resources that far more than replaced, in truth, what they used. And I am confident that we can do the same for our children. I would certainly rather have medicines and satellites and other technology than a few more billion tons of some rock or another."

It comes down to free choice, Boggs said. "We each can set our own economic time horizons. If we really think our grandchildren will be better off with shut-in oil wells than shares of IBM, we can buy them up and shut them in. But others should be free to make their own decisions.". . .

The Incoherence of Intergenerational Equity

It is fashionable in certain intellectual circles to argue, as does Edith Weiss, professor of international law at Georgetown University, that future generations have as much right to today's environmental resources as we do, and that we have no right to decide whether or not they should inherit their share of those rights.

Yet the idea that those not yet even conceived have tangible rights to resources is dubious to say the least. First, it is philosophically inconsistent. Those disembodied beings are said to have rights, yet the moment they are conceived, they are legally held to have no rights whatsoever. Leaving aside the ethics of abortion, to be consistent, those who defend the rights of future generations must by the same logic oppose abortion (a position few environmentalist activists hold, given their allegiance to population control). Once individuals are conceived, we do not maintain that they have a right to all the resources of their parents. If, for example, a retired couple spends $50,000 on a trip around the world, we do not argue that the couple has violated the resource rights of their children. Thus, individuals are said to have absolute resource rights before conception, no resource rights (indeed, not even the right to life) from conception to birth, and then only limited resource rights until death. If the theory of intergenerational equity is to be taken seriously, this obvious lurching arbitrariness will need to be expunged.

The concept of intergenerational equity, moreover, is hopelessly incoherent. If the choice to draw down resources is held exclusively by future generations, then are we not some previous generation's "future" generation? Why is the present generation bereft of that right? If the answer is that no generation has the right to deplete resources as long as another generation is on the horizon, then the logical implication is that no generation (save for the very last generation before the extinction of the species) will ever have a right to deplete any resource, no matter how urgent present needs may be. If only *one* generation (out of hundreds or even thousands) has the right to deplete resources, how is that "intergenerational equity"?

Furthermore, the notion of resource rights for future generations is premised on the argument that one has a "right" to forcibly take property from someone else in order to satisfy a personal need. Although that is an argument best left unexplored here, suffice it to say that such a claim is so expansive and fraught with peril that few philosophers have taken it seriously. . . .

Sustainable Development: An Intellectual Rorschach Test?

In sum, it is hard to overemphasize the wrong-headedness of sustainable development as a useful policy construct. As two distinguished scholars of the economic development—Partha Dasgupta and Karl-Goran Maler—point out, "most writings on sustainable development start from scratch and some proceed to get things hopelessly wrong. It would be difficult to find another field of research endeavor in the social sciences that displays such intellectual regress."

If sustainable development is the answer, what is the question? Society has managed to "sustain" development now for approximately 3,000 years without the guidance of green state planners. The result is not only a society that is both healthier and wealthier than any other in history, but a society with more natural resources at its disposal than ever before. One could reasonably argue that the best way to sustain development—or to maximize human welfare—is to protect economic liberty and confine state authority to protecting life, liberty, and property. That is, the best way of sustaining development is to reject "sustainable development."

Periodical Bibliography

The following articles have been selected to supplement the diverse views presented in this chapter.

Dennis T. Avery — "Population Pessimists Are More Than Merely Wrong," *American Outlook*, Winter 2000.

Ronald Bailey — "Earth Day, Then and Now," *Reason Online*, May 2000, www.reason.com.

Michel Bessières — "A Knife at the Throat of Half a Billion Farmers," *Unesco Courier*, January 2001.

B. Meredith Burke — "'Smart Growth' Ignores Many Harsh Truths," *Social Contract*, Summer 1999.

John Cairns Jr. — "Defining Goals and Conditions for a Sustainable World," *Environmental Health Perspectives*, November 1997.

John Cairns Jr. — "Malthus Revisited: Sustainability and the Denial of Limits," *Social Contract*, Spring 1998.

Ann Hironaka — "The Globalization of Environmental Protection: The Case of Environmental Impact Assessment," *International Journal of Comparative Sociology*, March 2002.

International Chamber of Commerce — "The World Business Organization," 2001, www.iccwbo.org.

Charles Leadbeater — "Globalization: Now the Good News," *New Statesman*, July 1, 2002.

Jerry Mander — "The Environment and Globalization," *IFG Bulletin*, Summer 2002.

Linda Martin — "Six Billion and Counting: Population Management at the Millennium," *Harvard International Review*, Fall 2000.

Philip Morse — "The Overpopulation Dilemma," *Human Quest*, May/June 1999.

David Pimentel and Marcia Pimentel — "Rising Populations, Diminishing Resources," *Forum for Applied Research and Public Policy*," Summer 1998.

Sheldon Richman — "It Just Ain't So!" *Freeman*, November 1998.

Michael E. Soulè — "Does Sustainable Development Help Nature?" *Wild Earth*, Winter 2000/2001.

Brian Tokar — "Beyond the Green Façade," *Toward Freedom*, May 1997.

Thad Williamson — "What an Environmentally Sustainable Economy Looks Like," *Dollars & Sense*, July/August 1999.

For Further Discussion

Chapter 1

1. Sarah A. Emerson asserts that technological innovation will permit oil companies to find and produce more and more oil. In contrast, Kenneth S. Deffeyes argues that oil production will decline because oil companies have already exhausted their technological know-how. After examining the evidence provided by both authors, do you think it is prudent to continue current oil consumption rates while depending on future technological innovations to find more oil? Or, do you think the United States should reduce its oil consumption and develop alternative energy sources? Please explain, citing specifics from the viewpoints.

2. Bjorn Lomborg supports his argument that food scarcity is not a serious problem by citing numerous examples of food production successes. However, Lester R. Brown backs up his argument that food will become scarcer by listing growing environmental problems—such as global water scarcity and depleted rangelands—that will reduce food supplies. Do you think that Lomborg's argument is undermined by his failure to mention the new contingencies that Lester outlines? Please explain your answer.

3. Marc Morano and Kent Washburn report that only 12.5 percent of the Amazon rain forest has been logged, which means that almost 90 percent of the forest is intact. Furthermore, they claim that such minimal destruction will have no adverse affect on the global climate. In contrast, Peter Bunyard argues that the 12.5 figure can provide a false sense of security. In fact, he contends, even that degree of deforestation could lead to serious climatic disruptions. Whose argument do you find more convincing? In general, do you think it is more advantageous to see the glass as half-full or half-empty in regards to environmental problems? Use specifics from the texts to develop your answer.

Chapter 2

1. Both the *Economist* and Vandana Shiva discuss the risks associated with genetically engineered food. However, whereas Shiva argues that genetically modified organisms (GMOs) should be abolished because of the risks they pose to the environment and human health, the *Economist* contends that such risks are speculative and claims that appropriate testing and oversight would guarantee the safety of GMOs. Which author do you think makes the more persuasive argument? Why?

2. Jonathan Dimbleby maintains that organic farming protects the environment by reducing the use of harmful pesticides and herbicides. In contrast, Dennis T. Avery argues that organic farming damages the environment because it produces less food per acre than conventional farming, necessitating the conversion of more wildlife habitat into cropland. After analyzing the evidence that each author provides to support his argument, which viewpoint do you find more convincing? Please explain your answer, citing specifics from the texts.

3. Ed Ayres, editorial director of the Worldwatch Institute, a research organization that analyzes global problems such as pollution, asserts that livestock agriculture harms the environment and threatens human health. The National Cattlemen's Beef Association, a trade association for America's one million cattle farmers and ranchers, claims that livestock agriculture benefits the environment and helps feed the world's people. How does knowing the credentials of both authors affect your evaluation of their respective arguments? Please explain.

Chapter 3

1. While Martin Bond claims that solar power is already producing significant amounts of electricity worldwide, William Booth contends that solar energy has yet to become an important energy source because it is still too expensive. Examine the evidence that each author provides to support his view. Which author do you find more convincing? Explain.

2. Douglas S. McGregor asserts that nuclear power is a safe and inexpensive way to produce electricity. In contrast, Karen Charman argues that nuclear energy is dangerous and expensive. After examining the evidence provided in the viewpoints, which author do you think makes the more persuasive argument? Please explain.

3. Birger T. Madsen claims that governments have helped the fossil-fuel industry establish an energy monopoly through legislation and subsidies. In order to break this monopoly, Madsen argues, governments worldwide should begin promoting clean energies such as wind power. Discuss the pros and cons of government involvement in energy production. In your opinion, should government be in the business of promoting one energy source over another? Please explain your answer.

4. Ty Cashman and Bret Logue recommend that local citizens urge their civic leaders to create "hydrogen cities." Discuss sev-

eral specific ideas about how you could help promote a hydrogen economy in your community.

5. David Ross asserts that energy from ocean waves will become a viable energy source. Does the fact that Ross has written several books on wave energy help or hurt his argument? Explain your answer.

Chapter 4

1. Werner Fornos contends that technological advancements cannot postpone indefinitely a global catastrophe stemming from human population growth. Conversely, Nicholas Eberstadt argues that human ingenuity will always enable people to create more natural resources. In your opinion, which author is more convincing? Evaluate the evidence that the authors provide to help develop your answer.

2. James M. Sheehan claims that globalized free trade protects global resources because the more money nations have, the more likely they will be to invest in environmental protections. However, Stanley Wood maintains that by the time many developing nations reap the financial benefits of increased trade, they will have irrevocably damaged the environment. Which author do you find more persuasive? Why?

3. Danja Van Der Veldt asserts that nations must adopt policies that encourage the preservation of resources so that future generations have at least as much as the present generation. In contrast, Jerry Taylor argues that conserving resources creates less income than exploiting them does and in the long run transmits less wealth to future generations. Examine each author's argument. In your opinion, who makes the stronger case? Explain.

Organizations to Contact

The editors have compiled the following list of organizations concerned with the issues debated in this book. The descriptions are derived from materials provided by the organizations. All have publications or information available for interested readers. The list was compiled on the date of publication of the present volume; names, addresses, phone and fax numbers, and e-mail and Internet addresses may change. Be aware that many organizations take several weeks or longer to respond to inquiries, so allow as much time as possible.

Center for Global Food Issues
PO Box 202, Churchville, VA 24421-0202
(540) 337-6354 • fax: (540) 337-8593
website: www.cgfi.org

The Center for Global Food Issues conducts research and analysis of agriculture and the environmental concerns surrounding food and fiber production. The Center uses its worldwide overview of food and farming to assess policies, improve farmers' understanding of the new globalized farm economy, and heighten awareness of the environmental impacts of various farming systems and food policies. It publishes the *Global Food Quarterly* and has made available many articles and papers on its website.

Competitive Enterprise Institute (CEI)
1001 Connecticut Ave. NW, Suite 1250, Washington, DC 20036
(202) 331-1010 • fax: (202) 331-0640
e-mail: info@cei.org • website: www.cei.org

The CEI encourages the use of the free market and private property rights to protect the environment. It advocates removing governmental regulatory barriers and establishing a system in which the private sector would be responsible for the environment. CEI's publications include the monthly newsletter *CEI Update*, the book *The True State of the Planet*, and the monograph "Federal Agriculture Policy: A Harvest of Environmental Abuse."

Environmental Defense Fund (EDF)
257 Park Ave. South, New York, NY 10010
(212) 505-2100 • fax: (212) 505-0892
website: www.edf.org

The fund is a public interest organization of lawyers, scientists, and economists dedicated to the protection and improvement of environmental quality and public health. It publishes the bimonthly *EDF Letter* and the report "Plastics Recycling: How Slow Can It Grow?"

Greenpeace USA
1436 U St. NW, Washington, DC 20009
(800) 326-0959 • fax: (202) 462-4507
e-mail: greenpeace@wdc.greenpeace.org
website: www.greenpeaceusa.org
Greenpeace opposes nuclear energy and the use of toxic chemicals and supports ocean and wildlife preservation. It uses controversial direct-action techniques and strives for media coverage of its actions in an effort to educate the public. It publishes the quarterly magazine *Greenpeace* and the books *Radiation and Health*, *Coastline*, and *The Greenpeace Book on Antarctica*.

Hudson Institute
Herman Kahn Center
5395 Emerson Way, PO Box 26-919, Indianapolis, IN 46226
(317) 545-1000 • fax: (317) 545-1384
e-mail: johnmc@hii.hudson.org • website: www.hudson.org
The Hudson Institute is a public policy research center whose members are elected from academia, government, and industry. The institute promotes the power of the free market and human ingenuity to solve environmental problems. Its publications include the monthly *Outlook* and the monthly policy bulletin *Foresight*.

International Food Policy Research Institute (IFPRI)
2033 K St. NW, Washington, DC 20006-1002
(202) 862-5600 • fax: (202) 467-4439
website: www.ifpri.org
The IFPRI is one of sixteen food and environmental research organizations known as the Future Harvest Centers. The centers, located around the world, conduct research in partnership with farmers, scientists, and policymakers to help alleviate poverty and increase food security while protecting the natural resource base. The mission of the institute is to identify and analyze policies for sustainably meeting the food needs of the developing world.

Natural Resources Defense Council (NRDC)
40 W. 20th St., New York, NY 10011
(212) 727-2700 • fax: (212) 727-1773
website: www.nrdc.org
The council is an environmental group composed of lawyers and scientists who conduct litigation and research on toxic waste and

other environmental hazards. The NRDC publishes pamphlets, brochures, reports, books, and the quarterly *Amicus Journal*.

Political Economy Research Center (PERC)
502 S. 19th Ave., Suite 211, Bozeman, MT 59715
(406) 587-9591
website: www.perc.org

PERC is a research and education foundation that focuses primarily on environmental and natural resource issues. It emphasizes the advantages of free markets and the importance of private property rights in environmental protection. PERC's publications include the quarterly newsletter *PERC Reports* and papers in the PERC Policy Series.

Rainforest Action Network (RAN)
221 Pine St., Suite 500, San Francisco, CA 94104
(415) 398-4404 • fax: (415) 398-2732
e-mail: rainforest@ran.org • website: www.ran.org

RAN works to preserve the world's rain forests through activism and education addressing the logging and importing of tropical timber, cattle ranching in rain forests, and the rights of indigenous rain forest peoples. RAN's publications include the monthly bulletin *Action Report* and the semiannual *World Rainforest Report*.

Reason Foundation
3415 S. Sepulveda Blvd., Suite 400, Los Angeles, CA 90034-6064
(310) 391-2245 • fax: (310) 391-4395
website: www.reason.org

The Reason Foundation is a libertarian public policy research organization. Its environmental research focuses on issues such as energy, global warming, and recycling. The foundation publishes the monthly magazine *Reason* and the books *Global Warming: The Greenhouse, White House, and Poor House Effect; The Case Against Electric Vehicle Mandates in California*; and *Solid Waste Recycling Costs—Issues and Answers*.

Stockholm Environment Institute (SEI)
Lilla Nygatan 1, Box 2142, S-103, 14 Stockholm, Sweden
46 8 412 1400 • fax: 46 8 723 0348
e-mail: postmaster@sei.se • website: www.sei.se

Headquartered in Sweden, the SEI is an internationally networked research institute that focuses on a variety of environmental issues, including climate change, energy use, and freshwater resources. The SEI publishes *SEI: An International Environment Bulletin* four times a year, *The Energy Report* twice a year, and *Environmental Perspectives* three times a year.

World Bank (IBRD)
Environment Department, 1818 H St. NW, Washington, DC 20433
(202) 473-1000 • fax: (202) 477-6391
website: www.worldbank.org
Formally known as the International Bank for Reconstruction and Development (IBRD), the World Bank seeks to reduce poverty and improve the standards of living of poor people around the world. It promotes sustainable growth and investments in developing countries through loans, technical assistance, and policy guidance. Many of the Bank's projects focus on agriculture, biodiversity, and energy. Its Environment Department publishes the periodicals *Environment Bulletin, Annual Report on the Environment,* and *Facing the Global Environment Change;* several series, including the Social Assessment Series and the Climate Change Series; and individual publications on environmental progress and desertification.

Worldwatch Institute
1776 Massachusetts Ave. NW, Washington, DC 20036-1904
(202) 452-1999 • fax: (202) 296-7365
e-mail: worldwatch@worldwatch.org
website: www.worldwatch.org
Worldwatch is a research organization that analyzes and calls attention to global problems, including environmental concerns such as the loss of cropland, forests, habitat, species, and water supplies. It compiles the annual *State of the World* anthology and publishes the bimonthly magazine *World Watch* and the Worldwatch Paper Series, which includes "Clearing the Air: A Global Agenda" and "The Climate of Hope: New Strategies for Stabilizing the World's Atmosphere."

Bibliography of Books

Jonathan H. Adler   *Environmentalism at the Crossroads.* Rockville, MD: Government Institutes, 1997.

Peter Asmus   *Reaping the Wind: How Mechanical Wizards, Visionaries, and Profiteers Helped Shape Our Energy Future.* Washington, DC: Island Press, 2000.

Ronald Bailey, ed.   *Earth Report 2000: Revisiting the True State of the Planet.* New York: McGraw-Hill, 2000.

Michael J. Balick, Elaine Elisabetsky, and Sarah A. Laird, eds.   *Medicinal Resources of the Tropical Forest: Biodiversity and Its Importance to Human Health.* New York: Columbia University Press, 1996.

Paul Ballonoff   *Energy: Ending the Never-Ending Crisis.* Washington, DC: Cato Institute, 1997.

Walton Beacham and Kirk H. Beetz, eds.   *Beacham's Guide to International Endangered Species.* Osprey, FL: Beacham Publishing, 1998.

Lester Brown   *Vital Signs.* New York: W.W. Norton, 2002.

Paul Brown   *Energy and Resources: Living for the Future.* Danbury, CT: Franklin Watts, 1998.

Michel Chossudovsky   *The Globalization of Poverty: Impacts of IMF and World Bank Reforms.* New York: Zed Books, 1999.

Michael J. Daley   *Nuclear Power: Promise or Peril?* Minneapolis, MN: Lerner Publications, 1997.

Kenneth S. Deffeyes   *Hubbert's Peak: The Impending World Oil Shortage.* Princeton, NJ: Princeton University Press, 2001.

Alan Thein Durning, Christopher D. Crowther, and Ellen W. Chu   *Misplaced Blame: The Real Roots of Population Growth.* Seattle, WA: Northwest Environment Watch, 1997.

Lloyd T. Evans   *Feeding the Ten Billion: Plants and Population Growth.* New York: Cambridge University Press, 1999.

Thomas L. Friedman   *The Lexus and the Olive Tree.* New York: Anchor Books, 2000.

Martha Honey   *Ecotourism and Sustainable Development: Who Owns Paradise?* Washington, DC: Island Press, 1999.

J. Robert Hunter   *Simple Things Won't Save the Earth.* Austin: University of Texas Press, 1997.

Joshua Karliner	*The Corporate Planet: Ecology and Politics in the Age of Globalization*. San Francisco: Sierra Club Books, 1997.
David S. Landes	*The Wealth and Poverty of Nations: Why Some Nations Are So Rich and Some So Poor*. New York: W.W. Norton, 1998.
Frances Moore Lappe, Joseph Collins, and Peter Rosset	*World Hunger: Twelve Myths*. New York: Grove Press, 1998.
James Larminie and Andrew Dick	*Fuel Cells Explained*. Etobicoke, Ontario: John Wiley and Sons, 2000.
Bjom Lomborg	*The Skeptical Environmentalist: Measuring the Real State of the World*. New York: Cambridge University Press, 1998.
Jerry Mander and Edward Goldsmith, eds.	*The Case Against the Global Economy*. San Francisco: Sierra Club Books, 1996.
Tomas Markvart, ed.	*Solar Electricity*. Etobicoke, Ontario: John Wiley and Sons, 2000.
Robert C. Morris	*The Environmental Case for Nuclear Power: Economic, Medical, and Political*. St. Paul, MN: Paragon House, 2000.
Robert A. Ristinen and Jack I. Kraushaar	*Energy and the Environment*. Etobicoke, Ontario: John Wiley and Sons, 1998.
Clifford J. Sherry	*Endangered Species: A Reference Handbook*. Santa Barbara, CA: ABC-CLIO, 1998.
Vandana Shiva	*Stolen Harvest: The Hijacking of the Global Food Supply*. Cambridge, MA: South End Press, 1999.
Robert Snedden	*Energy Alternatives*. Westport, CT: Heinemann Library, 2001.
George Soros	*The Crisis of Global Capitalism*. New York: PublicAffairs, 1998.
Thomas T. Struhsaker	*Ecology of an African Rain Forest: Logging in Kibale and the Conflict Between Conservation and Exploitation*. Gainesville: University Press of Florida, 1997.
United Nations	*The World at Six Billion*. New York: United Nations Population Division, 1999.
Adam S. Weinbert, David N. Pellow, and Allan Schnailberg	*Urban Recycling and the Search for Sustainable Development*. Princeton, NJ: Princeton University Press, 2000.
Worldwatch Institute	*State of the World 2000*. New York: W.W. Norton, 2000.

Index

South China Sea, oil exploration in, 22
starvation
  in developing world, 40
  UN definition of, 40–41
  see also malnutrition
Stott, Philip, 47, 53
superweeds, 73–74
surveys. See polls
sustainable development. See
  development, sustainable
Sustainable Fisheries Act (1996), 16

Tapchan, 155
Tararua Wind Farm (New Zealand),
  143
Tauxe, Robert, 89
Taylor, Jerry, 202
Taylor, John, 200
technology, petroleum
  advances in, have already been felt,
    21
    con, 205–206
  is lowering costs of oil, 28
Teller, Edward, 130
Three Mile Island accident, 130, 133
  victims of, 138
Twain, Mark, 10, 12

Union of Concerned Scientists, 69–70
United Nations
  Commission on Economic
    Development (UNCED), 203–204
  Development Program (UNDP), 66
  ecotourism and, 161
  Intergovernmental Panel on Climate
    Change, 148
  resolutions against overfishing by,
    15–16
United States
  efficiency of beef production in, 99
  nuclear power generation in, 131
  peak of oil production in, 19
  solar energy goals of, 112
  use of parabolic trough reflectors in,
    110
  water shortages in, 12

urbanization, 168
USA Today (newspaper), 138

Van Der Veldt, Danja, 194
Verfaillie, Hendrik, 69

Wakeland, Jim, 119
Warford, Jeremy, 204
Washburn, Kent, 50
Washington Times (newspaper), 137
water
  availability of, on Earth, 10–11
  extent of growing deficiency in, 167
  livestock agriculture is wasteful of, 95
    con, 100
  manufacturing and processing uses
    of, 101
  privatization of supplies of, 191
wave energy
  is a promising energy source, 153–57
  potential energy from, 154
  technical problems with, 156–57
Weiss, Edith, 208
Wells, Alan, 155
wildlife, cattle production contributes
  to, 102–103
Williams, Robert, 149
wind power
  costs of, 144–45
  public perception of, 143
  use of, should be increased, 140–45
wind turbines, efficiency of, 141
Wood, Megan Epler, 161
Wood, Stanley, 187
World Bank
  emphasis on education by, 197–98
  sustainable development and, 195–96
World Commission on Environment
  and Development, 195
World Health Organization, 33
World Trade Organization, 190

Yang, Maw Cheng, 177
Yucca Mountain storage site, 135–37

Zimmerman, Susan, 137